BLACK ENTERPRISE
LESSONS
FROM THE
TOP

Black Enterprise books provide useful information on a broad spectrum of business and general-interest topics, including entrepreneurship, personal and business finance, and career development. They are designed to meet the needs of the vital and growing African-American business market and to provide the information and resources that will help African-Americans achieve their goals. The books are written by and about African-American professionals and entrepreneurs, and they have been developed with the assistance of the staff of *Black Enterprise*, the premier African-American business magazine.

The series currently includes the following books:

Lessons from the Top: Success Strategies from America's Leading Black CEOs
by Derek T. Dingle

Black Enterprise Guide to Starting Your Own Business
by Wendy Beech

The Millionaires' Club: How to Start and Run Your Own Investment Club—and Make Your Money Grow!
by Caroline M. Brown

The Black Enterprise Guide to Investing
by James A. Anderson

Against All Odds: Ten Inspiring Stories of Successful African-American Entrepreneurs
by Wendy Harris

Take a Lesson: Contemporary Achievers on How They Made It and What They Learned Along the Way
by Caroline Clarke

Black Enterprise Guide to Building Your Career
by Cassandra Hayes

Black Enterprise Guide to Bridging the Digital Divide: Strategies for African American Entrepreneurs
by Bernadette Williams

Wealth Building Journal: A Day-by-Day Journey to a Brighter Future, a Better You
by the Editors of *Black Enterprise* Magazine

BLACK ENTERPRISE
LESSONS
FROM THE
TOP

Success Strategies from America's Leading Black CEOs

DEREK T. DINGLE

JOHN WILEY & SONS, INC.

*To my mother, Mattie, for her unwavering love and support;
and to my late grandfather, John Emory Spruill,
a man of quiet determination and honor.*

CONTENTS

v

FOREWORD

One took a culture defined by rhymes and beats born to the streets and created a multimedia empire of music and fashion. Another took a failed cable channel proposal and converted it into a history-making initial public offering on the New York Stock Exchange. A third made the notion of economic self-determination real by creating one of the nation's most successful community-focused banking institutions. Still another decided to recast the image of an entire people, and in so doing built a publishing and beauty-products empire that markets some of the most recognized brand names in American industry.

They are the Titans of the Black Enterprise 100s, and for most Americans, theirs may be the greatest stories of American industry never told—until now. You can be sure that the book you now hold in your hands—the first in a series to be produced by *Black Enterprise* in partnership with John Wiley & Sons—is unlike any you have ever read before.

In the beginning, there was *Black Enterprise*. When I launched this national business magazine in August of 1970, I dared to propose that African Americans were prepared to make great contributions and reap greater rewards, as enterpreneurs, executives, and professionals in

American industry. The publishing of the first issue of *Black Enterprise* signaled the dawn of a new age for African Americans, marked by the birth of America's first black professional class of business owners and corporate leaders. The emergence of captains of industry, business leaders whose vision, gift for leadership, innovative ideas, and indomitable spirit place them head and shoulders above the rest, was inevitable. For the past three decades, *Black Enterprise* has provided them with critical business information while chronicling their achievements.

In 1973, *Black Enterprise* became the first to quantify the growth and development of the largest black-owned American companies, when we published the first ever "Top 100 Black Businesses" ranking. This list, like the magazine that created it, was a manifestation of the civil rights victories of the 1960s and the "Black Capitalism" initiatives that were the hallmark of the presidential administration of President Richard M. Nixon, Today, that original list of top 100 businesses has evolved into the B.E. 100s, including lists of the nation's largest industrial/service companies, auto dealerships, commercial banks and thrifts, insurance companies, advertising agencies, and investment banks. More importantly, the personalities who have led B.E. 100s companies past and present—Arthur G. Gaston, Berry Gordy, Herman J. Russell, Nathan Conyers, Jr., Henry Parks, and Reginald F. Lewis, the families Gardner and Sutton, and, of course, the Johnsons: John, Robert, George, and Al (no relation to one another)—have become legend in the *Black Enterprise* universe, synonymous with excellence and innovation against the odds.

And yet, too many Americans, including those who are students and even fans of success stories in American business, are unfamiliar with these giants and ignorant about the contributions they and their companies have made and do make to American industry and life. As our gaze focuses beyond the threshold of a new millennium, the mission of this book, as it continues to be for our magazine, is to rectify that.

This is a book of African American success stories,

true; but, more importantly, it chronicles uniquely American, universally human triumphs. They reflect a more truthful image of the reality and the potential of American opportunity, an image largely ignored or grossly distorted by so-called general-audience business books and magazines. Their stories will instruct, inspire, illuminate, and, hopefully, motivate you to build on their success—or, better yet, provide you with a tool to further the next generation of captains of industry of all races and both genders.

It was Victor Hugo who observed that there is nothing more powerful than an idea whose time has come. Well, it's been a long time coming, but it's here, and you have it: the powerful ideas of 11 great business leaders—the Titans of the B.E. 100s.

> —EARL G. GRAVES
> Chairman and CEO of Earl G. Graves Ltd.
> Founder, Editor, and Publisher of *Black
> Enterprise* Magazine

INTRODUCTION

Money has no color. If you can build a better mousetrap, it
won't matter whether you're black or white. People will buy it.
—A. G. Gaston

Who runs the nation's largest black-owned companies? Bootstrap entrepreneurs. Rugged empire builders.
Master deal makers. Innovative inventors. High-risk
venturers.

This self-made group of African Americans have been
the vanguard of an entrepreneurial revolution. Achieving
despite lack of capital, diminished access, and outright
racism, they used imagination and drive to seize opportunities and break barriers. For some, their path has meant
employment, training, and advancement for large numbers of African Americans. Others have performed in the
American business mainstream as well as on the world
stage. All of them, however, stand among black America's
wealthiest and most powerful players.

The ascension of the B.E. 100s—the companies that
Black Enterprise magazine has ranked and chronicled for
more than 25 years—is reflective of the vision and drive of

these entrepreneurs, and their contributions have been just as significant as those of Time Inc.'s Henry Luce, Microsoft's Bill Gates, Cable News Network (CNN)'s Ted Turner, News Corporation's Rupert Murdoch, Trump Castle's Donald Trump, and Republic Industries' Wayne Huizenga. These companies have created such brands as *Ebony* magazine, the Motown sound, Parks sausages ("More Parks' sausages, Mom!"), the *Essence* woman, and BET (Black Entertainment Television).

The B.E. 100s represent, in many ways, the economic evolution of African Americans since World War II. The first step in the effort for black equality was driven largely by the Civil Rights Movement, which led to the social and legal reforms of the 1950s and 1960s. Next, the passage of the Civil Rights Act of 1964 and the Voting Rights Act of 1965, which eliminated such barriers to political activity as the poll tax and literacy test, gave rise to the increase in black political strength with the election of blacks to city hall and Congress in the late 1960s and 1970s. Those events were followed by the propulsion of black economic power in which African Americans gained an opportunity to amass wealth and a real opportunity to achieve the American Dream that had been elusive for so long. In the 1980s and 1990s, blacks, who had gained access to the nation's leading universities and colleges as well as major corporations, leveraged their education and experience to acquire and finance new companies through such instruments as public offerings, leveraged buyouts, and junk bonds, as well as to develop enterprises through emerging technologies.

The best and brightest first received national recognition in the June 1973 issue of *Black Enterprise*, which featured the inaugural listing of "The Nation's Top 100 Black Businesses," or the "Top 100." The ranking, like the publication that created it, was an outgrowth of Black Capitalism, the program that was ironically developed by Republican President Richard Nixon. In March 1969, Nixon signed Executive Order 11458, which directed the Commerce Department to coordinate the federal government's programs "which affect or may contribute to the establishment, preservation and strengthening of minority business enterprise." The new mandate spawned the Office of Minority Business Enterprise (known today as the Minority Business Development Agency, or MBDA), public venture capital firms, and federal set-asides. Not to say that there were not examples of black entrepreneurship before the Nixon executive order, but it gave many entrepreneurs the ability to grow beyond mom-and-pop status and eventually operate on Wall Street as well as Main Street.

Black businesses have shown significant growth over the past quarter of a century. The original Top 100, which included industrial, service, and professional businesses, had total annual sales of $473.4 million and employed a total of 9267 people. Over the years, the rapid growth in the number of black-owned auto dealerships in the nation as well as professionally trained financiers gave rise to the B.E. 100s—the B.E. Industrial/Service 100 and the B.E. Auto Dealer 100. Other lists under the banner include the B.E. Top 20 Advertising Agencies, the B.E. Top 25 Banks, the B.E. Top 10 Insurance Companies, and the B.E. Top 15 Investment Banks. Today, these companies have revenues exceeding $14 billion and more than 55,000 employees on their payrolls.

These concerns have served as a barometer for black business development. From the inception of the rankings, the chief executive officers (CEOs) have represented three generations of entrepreneurs. A. G. Gaston, who was named *Black Enterprise*'s Entrepreneur of the Century in 1992 at the ripe age of 100, built a complex of companies in Birmingham, Alabama, at a time when it was considered the most segregated city in America. He launched Booker T. Washington Insurance Company in 1932 and Citizens Federal Savings Bank in 1957 to serve black consumers shunned by white institutions. To this day, these companies remain mainstays on the B.E. Top Insurance 10 and the B.E. Top Bank 25, respectively. In addition to these companies, his empire included a funeral parlor, a construction company, a drugstore, and radio stations. He said that becoming wealthy was "accidental," filling voids in the black community. He did not let racism or lack of access stop him from achieving his goal.

In the June 1992 issue of *Black Enterprise*, one of his last interviews, Gaston asserted:

> *Money has no color. If you can build a better mouse-trap, it won't matter whether you're black or white. People will buy it.*

Others followed his advice of self-reliance and ingenuity. Bootstrappers who launched their enterprises before the Civil Rights Movement include John H. Johnson, who used $500 in 1942 to start a series of national magazines for African Americans, including *Ebony* and *Jet,* and build a $325 million global communications conglomerate; Herman J. Russell, who used $125 in savings as the first step in creating the nation's largest black-owned construction firm; and C. H. James, who developed a food distribution business in 1883 that is now run by his great-grandson C. H. "Chuck" James III, a Wharton M.B.A. who turned the concern into an international vendor for major corporations.

The further growth of the B.E. 100s can be attributed, in part, to government policy that helped black business owners gain access to financing and contracts in the 1970s and 1980s. The CEOs who started companies during this era include such standouts as former gridiron star Mel Farr, who created a $573 million automotive fiefdom by stitching together Ford, Toyota, Volkswagen, and Mazda franchises to create a national network of dealerships; Byron Lewis, who produced one of the nation's largest black-owned advertising agencies and some of the most innovative commercials in magazines and on television; and Percy Sutton, the Manhattan borough president and mayoral candidate, who developed a chain of profitable radio stations.

The B.E. 100s faced major challenges with the erosion of affirmative action in the public and private sectors that was pushed by the Reagan and Bush Administrations and backed by decisions of a conservative Supreme Court. These anti–affirmative action initiatives continue today, most notably in California and the state of Washington.

During the late 1980s and 1990s, CEOs of the largest black-owned companies overcame obstacles through a tradition of tenacity and ingenuity as well as the implementation of innovative financing techniques and technology. The rise of the financial entrepreneur was highlighted by the landmark deal orchestrated by the late deal maker Reginald F. Lewis. In 1987, he structured the $985 million leveraged buyout of TLC Beatrice International Foods, which created the first B.E. 100s company to gross more than $1.8 billion. The transaction raised the bar for black entrepreneurs to make inroads into the mainstream financial community to buy and build businesses. Such developments included Robert Johnson's transformation of BET Holdings, Inc., from a single cable network to an entertainment monolith that became the first black-owned business listed on the New York Stock Exchange. Another entrepreneur, Don H. Barden, successfully used high-yield bonds to create a mammoth gaming enterprise.

Another aspect of the B.E. 100s has been the preservation and modification of generational businesses, a relatively new phenomenon for black enterprises on a grand scale. And these companies have not only had an impact on mainstream business but have, in fact, created national trends. Motown Industries, which was the No. 1 B.E. 100s company for 13 years, was responsible for driving the pop music industry in the 1960s and 1970s with its legendary Motown sound. In the 1980s and 1990s, Russell Simmons followed suit, revolutionizing the music industry by introducing hip-hop to the world through his Def Jam Records subsidiary.

But whether they are bootstrappers, innovators, or financial engineers, there are common traits shared by the business titans featured on the pages of *Black Enterprise* and in this book. The attributes include:

Vision. All of the CEOs interviewed have the ability to

envision products and services that filled a void in the consumer market and, in turn, revolutionized and advanced whole industries.

Order. All of them know their sectors intimately and have tightly structured their organizations. These chief executives have the ability to find talented employees and advisers to lift their concern to the next level.

Focus. Many of these entrepreneurs have built their companies from the ground up and have been relentless in doing so. Their lives are seamless, including family in their business and financial activities.

Passion. These CEOs *love* the companies that they run and become energized by new ventures—and adventures.

In the course of 25 years, this new breed of entrepreneurs have become rich, prominent, and powerful. They were able to do so because they kept their enterprises in step with—and, in some cases, ahead of—the times. On the following pages, meet the individuals who represent profound transformations in global business and spectacular realizations of the American Dream.

JOHN H. JOHNSON: JOHNSON PUBLISHING COMPANY, INC.

The Pioneer

JOHN H. JOHNSON

Age: 80.

Birthplace: Arkansas City, Arkansas.

Marital Status: Married 58 years to wife, Eunice, the company's secretary-treasurer.

Children: One daughter, Linda Johnson Rice, 40, serves as president and chief operating officer. (One son, John H. Johnson, Jr., died in 1981 of sickle-cell anemia.)

Education: Attended the University of Chicago and Northwestern University.

Entity: Johnson Publishing Company, Inc.

Established: 1942.

Corporate Headquarters: Chicago, Illinois.

Products: *Ebony, Jet,* and *Ebony South Africa* magazines; Fashion Fair Cosmetics; Supreme Beauty Products; Ebony Fashion Fair (world's largest traveling fashion show); Johnson Book Publishing Division; American Black Achievement Awards.

Annual Sales: $361 million.

Number of Employees: 2677.

First Job: Newspaper delivery boy.

First Career Move: Editing an in-house newsletter for Supreme Life Insurance Company.

First Business: Publisher of now defunct *Negro Digest.*

Heroes: His mother, Gertrude Johnson Williams.

Johnson's Basics: *The most important thing a manager can learn is the ability to analyze a situation and quickly think his way out of it.*

On Managing: *I believe in hands-on, hands-in, hands-wrapped-around management, in which you delegate freely and check up on people every day.*

On Capitalization: *I've never let the inability to get capital keep me from growing and surviving. . . . If you believe in something, to have the commitment is really more important than having the money.*

1

JOHN H. JOHNSON: JOHNSON PUBLISHING COMPANY, INC.

The Pioneer

I run scared every business day and use every legal means necessary to survive and grow.

Icon.

Scribes have always inappropriately used the label to characterize America's latest business hero. Too often, they tag it onto a young Icarus who later comes crashing down to Earth after some ephemeral success, or to a so-called Master of the Universe with the ability to descend from a corporate perch by way of a golden parachute.

Try growing up a poor, black child of the Deep South, raised by a determined, God-fearing mother after your father dies before your seventh birthday. Move to a Midwestern metropolis and spend your teenage years, lean and hungry during the height of the Depression and forced to subsist on welfare. With all the strikes against you and virtually penniless, conjure up a dream of launching a monthly publication. Then, despite the obstacles—and, in most cases, because of them—transform that vision into an empire that produces magazines, radio and television programs, insurance, cosmetics, hair-care products, and fashion shows. Wealth, power, and success enable you to conduct business around the globe, sit on the boards of the nation's largest corporations, and consult with nine U.S. presidents. That's a life worthy of living legend status.

John Harold Johnson achieved it all.

Without the intervention of banks, the Small Business Administration, set-asides, or rich uncles, he built Chicago-based Johnson Publishing Company, Inc., into the largest self-made black business in the world. Even the rich and powerful dub him "The Godfather" for steadily growing his vast enterprise for 57 years, through recessions, industrial revolutions, and personal tribulations.

Johnson earned the immodest sobriquet not because the old-fashioned rugged individualist channeled anger and rejection into a net worth of more than $200 million. He forged an institution that has touched the lives of three generations of African Americans. For 54 years, *Ebony* magazine, the company's flagship, has graced the coffee tables of black households, serving as a national messenger of African American achievement with its glossy coverage of celebrated personalities and historic events. Since 1951, *Jet*, the weekly digest, has provided readers with a concise compilation of news and gossip, complete with celebrity and society photos and a hubba-hubba centerfold of a bikini-clad beauty. To this day, faithful readers say, "If it wasn't covered in *Jet*, it didn't happen in black America." Ebony Fashion Fair, which debuted in 1958, offered African Americans their first opportunity to witness black elegance and style on a runway. Until the introduction of Fashion Fair cosmetics in 1974, black women were not able to find makeup to satisfy their kaleidoscope of hues and skin textures.

Some would assert that the evolution of these ventures was a function of zeitgeist. This may be true, but Johnson had the moxie to conceive them and a genius for timing. He knew black people wanted to read about their achievements, see photographs of their children's weddings and cotillions, buy beauty and grooming aids designed specifically for their features, and get a glimpse of glamour. He went through the pain, humiliation, and exhilaration of blazing trails, transforming lives, and uplifting a people.

Along the way, he figured out a way to make loads of money doing it.

He still does.

In 1997, Johnson Publishing grossed $361 million, a staggering growth rate of 1400 percent since the company first appeared on the *Black Enterprise* list of the nation's 100 largest black-owned businesses in 1973. Johnson maintains that he reached this pinnacle by being "poor, ambitious, and scared"—and consistent. In fact, the only difference between his mode of operation today and five decades ago is that he is no longer broke.

> *I tend to be cautiously optimistic and I never get over-confident. I run scared every business day and use every legal means necessary to survive and grow.*

You can bet that as long as he is breathing, JPC will always be John Johnson's company. Even when he is not there, his presence is palpable, felt from the lobby to the top floor of his corporate headquarters, an 11-story structure of bleached concrete and glass that remains the only black-owned and -constructed building in downtown Chicago.

At 80, looking more like 60, he's still fiercely competitive, clocking 14-hour days—although he no longer spends his weekends in the office. Entrepreneurial electricity courses through his compact frame. He operates from a top-floor suite that includes a workout room, a barber's chair, a kitchen, sleeping quarters, and what's known as the "give 'em hell" room, a woodshed of sorts for errant employees. Johnson is not one of those CEOs content to stay tucked away atop his tower. In fact, he manages by roaming, dropping in on employees at a moment's notice. It's all part of what he calls "hands-on, hands-in, hands-wrapped-around management, in which you delegate freely and check up on people every day." Over the years, he has periodically sat in his lobby to ensure the punctuality of employees. He runs editorial meetings, approving and rejecting story ideas. And, to this day, his signature can be found on every company check.

His style has earned him the well-deserved reputation of being one of the toughest bosses in American business. His expectations have always been crystal clear and bluntly stated: "[If] people did not do the work, they were dismissed, period." Naysayers don't last, either. Just ask the first person he ever fired, who was let go for telling Johnson that *Ebony* would not succeed. When the boss handed over the pink slip, he maintained, "I'm too insecure about [*Ebony* succeeding] myself to have somebody around telling me that I can't do it."

On the other hand, he's retained a cadre of trusted employees for decades—developing a list of what it takes to keep valued personnel happy. With such enticements as furnishing vice presidents with leased Cadillacs and charging employees a mere $1 for a lunch that, on occasion, includes steak and lobster, it's a list that would make even Oprah, the grande dame of job perks, proud.

Preferring to fly solo, Johnson never puts himself in a position where other people tell him what to do. In the early 1960s, Johnson turned down an ambassadorship offered by President John F. Kennedy "because you have no power. You're never in control of your destiny." Nor does he want outsiders telling him how to run his business. For that reason, the company has no board. He does, however, consult with his wife of 58 years, Eunice, who is secretary-treasurer, and his 40-year-old daughter, Linda Johnson Rice, president and chief operating officer.

Johnson has long rejected the textbook tenets of business, unless they happen to coincide with his own approach. His may not be the way of the moment, but he couldn't care less. Johnson does things the Johnson way—conventional wisdom be damned—and it has worked.

I have served on a lot of boards and heard a lot about five-year plans throughout the years. Five-year plans may sound good on Wall Street but I haven't seen many that have worked. I don't think anyone is smart enough to see five years into the future. I have always developed a yearly plan and monitored it on a month-to-month basis.

Proud. Direct. Smart. If you see Johnson in a photo or at a public ceremony, he wears the same stoic, determined expression that he did as a kid. His comments tend to be blunt, and, when agitated, traces of his Arkansas roots resonate in the timbre of his voice. Relaxed, he peppers his conversations with humorous anecdotes and is quick to burst into laughter at the telling of his own favorite stories.

Symbols are important to him, as they are to many of his generation. Stored in the corporate garage is a dusty, 15-year-old Rolls-Royce that he has driven only three times. He didn't care about driving the Rolls, he explains. He just wanted to own it.

Lesson #1: Never Forget Mama

In recalling his road from bucolic Arkansas City, Arkansas, to the tony heights of Lake Shore Drive in Chicago, Johnson begins not with his own accomplishments, but with those of his late mother. Widowed as a young adult, Gertrude Johnson resolved not to let poverty or Jim Crow diminish the aspirations she held for her only child. A domestic with no more than a third-grade education herself, Gertrude was determined that John would hit the books and reap the rewards that eluded her. He was going to be somebody.

Back then, it was an audacious notion. Tiny Arkansas City didn't have a high school and there wasn't enough money to send him away to continue his education. So, she made her son repeat the eighth grade while she saved enough money to move them to Chicago.

Although the bustling urban hub gave the 15-year-old Johnson access to better schools, it didn't offer much in the way of economic opportunity. The Great Depression gripped the nation, and his family, like millions of others, was caught in the vise. Gertrude, who remarried, couldn't

find domestic work, and his stepfather searched fruit-
lessly for odd jobs. With no other options, the family went
on welfare.

Johnson was shamed by the public handouts. The humiliation of those three years still burns in his memory.
So do bright memories of Gertrude Johnson's zeal.

> *My mother had the greatest influence on my life. She
> gave me hope that one day, somehow, I would tri-
> umph. She gave me patience, which is absolutely nec-
> essary in business.*

Johnson put his scholarly energies into DuSable High
School. A voracious reader, he adopted new heroes from
books on such historic figures as Booker T. Washington
and Frederick Douglass. His passion for journalism led to
the editorship of the school newspaper. Outside of the
classroom, he spent hours improving himself by reading
Dale Carnegie's *How to Win Friends and Influence People*
and rehearsing speeches in front of the mirror.

The push for personal and academic excellence earned
him a partial scholarship to the University of Chicago.
The award, however, paid only $200 of his tuition, not
nearly enough to cover his expenses for the year.

He found the answer to his financial woes at an Urban
League luncheon recognizing local students for their academic achievements. As one of the honorees, he listened
to the keynote speaker, who talked about the importance
of education, tenacity, and setting goals. The lecturer was
Harry Pace, president of Supreme Liberty Life Insurance
Company, the largest black-owned business in Chicago.

After the speech, Johnson rushed up to the podium
and introduced himself. As the two talked, Johnson told
Pace of his plight. Impressed, Pace offered him a part-
time job flexible enough for him to attend college. He
leaped at the chance and the much-needed paycheck. In
the fall of 1936, the 18-year-old high school graduate began his professional life as a $25-a-week office worker.

> *It was a turning point because I had an opportunity
> there to observe black people running a business. Up*

to that point, I had seen lawyers, ministers, doctors, but I had never seen a successful black businessman. And here I was working for a company which was the largest black business in the North at the time, and I saw men making big decisions. I saw them moving around with dignity and with security, and it inspired me. It made me realize that my career could be in business, and that success was possible.

Lesson #2: Start Small, Aim High

In 1939, Johnson quit college to accept a full-time job as editor of Supreme Life's employee magazine. The job required him to scan newspapers and magazines and write a summary of events in black America each week. He showed the publication to friends, who became interested in receiving the same information.

The budding entrepreneur quickly became smitten with the idea of starting such a publication—his version of *Reader's Digest.*

Johnson was to become such a business colossus that it's hard to believe he didn't start out with the goal of ruling the world. He foresaw the advantages of climbing a hill instead of scaling a mountain. He still does.

I always advise young people to dream small dreams, because small dreams can be achieved, and once you achieve a small dream and a small success, it gives you confidence to go on to the next big step. They must understand that a grocery store can indeed develop into a chain of supermarkets. Entrepreneurship is personal. It is what you can do almost by yourself. When I started out, I did not see the company the way it is today. And I think if I did, I probably would have been so overwhelmed, with my meager resources, that I wouldn't have started it.

He needed cash for his unformed enterprise. First, he went to Chicago's First National Bank. Within minutes of entering the lobby, he was shown out by loan officers who contemptuously referred to him as "boy" and informed him that the institution would never lend money to blacks.

He was bitter, but he took a page from Dale Carnegie: *Don't get mad, get smart.*

Johnson set his sights on the black community, trying to persuade influential African Americans to buy as much as a half interest in the publication for $1000. He was turned down cold and advised that he would be better off as a teacher or insurance salesman. Down to his last few bucks, he hopped on a train to New York to meet with Roy Wilkins of the National Association for the Advancement of Colored People. Wilkins was the editor of the NAACP magazine, *The Crisis*, the only viable black monthly magazine at the time. Wilkins looked him square in the face and said, "Save your money, young man. Save your energy. Save yourself a lot of disappointment."

Bucking that advice, Johnson turned to the most influential person in his life, his mother. He persuaded her to put up her furniture as collateral for a $500 loan. She agreed, praying that his venture would pan out.

Next, he talked to his benefactor, Harry Pace. The black executive not only encouraged him, but also let Johnson use Supreme Life's mailing list of 20,000 policyholders to solicit $2 subscriptions.

> *I remember the letter very well. It said, "A good friend of yours told me that you would be interested in a new magazine that I'm bringing out at such and such a time. This friend told me that you were a person who would like to keep up with current events, who liked to be well-informed, and that because of this, you would be interested in this magazine." About 3000 people answered the letter and many of them, after having written their check, would ask, "Oh, by the way, what friend told you about me?" Actually, no friend told me.*

The scheme enabled him to raise $6000 in start-up capital without putting up a single cent of his own money. Johnson operated the Negro Digest Publishing Company in the corner of the law library of Earl Dickerson, an attorney who rented space in the Supreme Life building. There, he drafted and sent out letters for the right to publish certain stories from black newspapers and white periodicals. Eunice, his social-worker wife of one year, stuffed envelopes and helped with editorial and circulation functions.

On November 1, 1942, Johnson launched *Negro Digest*. His initial print run was 5000 copies. Although he had 3000 subscribers, he wanted to sell the remaining 2000 copies on newsstands. Hoping to increase the publication's exposure, Johnson went to the biggest distributor in Chicago. He was told that they "didn't carry colored books because colored books didn't sell."

Johnson responded by formulating his own first theory of management:

> *The most important thing a manager can learn is the ability to analyze a situation and quickly think his way out of it.*

He quickly reasoned that if he could stoke demand for *Negro Digest*, then the distributor would be forced to carry it. He rounded up 30 or so friends from the insurance company and sent them to newsstands throughout Chicago's South Side to ask for copies of the publication. When numbers of customers requested *Negro Digest*, the dealers called the distributor seeking this hot new commodity.

Now, he needed to make the magazine a bona fide success. If not, *Negro Digest* would surely lose its distribution. Once again, he assembled his friends. "I want you to go out and buy *Negro Digest*," he told them. "Don't worry about the money. I'll give you the cash to pay for it."

The strategy worked in Chicago, but Johnson needed to develop a national strategy to get the publication sold in other cities.

> *If you can't gain help from others, you have to figure out what you can do by yourself to get what you want. It was not my original intention to start a distribution company. I had to do it in order to grow.*

Here's how it worked: Johnson would find an agent to distribute the magazine, but usually that person didn't have money or credit. Johnson would set up a local account under his company's name and instruct the bank that money could be deposited but not withdrawn. At the end of each month, the agent would keep a share of the money and deposit the rest. The bank would then notify Johnson whether the money was deposited. If his agent came up short, he would not ship any more magazines. In the South, where it was impossible to get a black magazine on newsstands because of Jim Crow laws, he developed a network of salesmen who sold the publication on buses, streetcars, and even in cotton fields. Within eight months, circulation of *Negro Digest* grew to 50,000 copies.

All successful start-up entrepreneurs have to have the stomach for two things: begging for money and asking for favors, regardless of how high they have to climb up the food chain. The brash Johnson decided to make his presence known at the White House.

In 1943, he wrote to the First Lady, Eleanor Roosevelt, asking her to write an article. She replied that she didn't have time. Johnson was undeterred. Discovering that she was planning a visit to Chicago, he asked her to dictate a column to him while she was there. She agreed. When the issue hit the newsstands with Eleanor Roosevelt's take on race relations, *Negro Digest*'s circulation doubled overnight.

Lesson #3: If You Can't Go through the Front Door, Use a Side Entrance

The sales of *Negro Digest* rose as America entered a new era. The end of World War II brought veterans, black and white, home to find jobs and start families. Their return signaled the promise of affluence. In 1945, Johnson, all of 27, was being drawn into exploring new frontiers.

At the urging of two of his top freelance writers, he studied a proposal for a magazine called *Jive*. It would be an entertainment publication targeted at the emerging hip set.

At first, Johnson was not totally sold on the concept but agreed to invest in the venture as a way of retaining valuable talent. He told them that if each of them ponied up $1000, he would launch the magazine as a partnership and split profits three ways. When the two were unable to come up with the dough, Johnson decided to go it alone, putting his own spin on their concept.

Through informal research, the young publisher found that large numbers of blacks were buying *Life*, the popular pictorial magazine, from newsstands on Chicago's South Side. These readers would be far more interested in a similar publication that revealed the positive aspects of black life. If *Life* showed the so-called American Century, then his publication would unveil the African American equivalent. On Eunice's suggestion, Johnson christened the magazine *Ebony*, after the fine, dark wood from the tropical trees of Africa.

In an interview during *Ebony*'s 40th anniversary in 1985, he explained why he decided to move forward with the publication:

> *First, I think the timing was right. Secondly, I think the market was ready. Thirdly, I think I was able to learn from mistakes. I recognized that if you are going to travel a long distance, you can't burden yourself with a heavy load. I went in for the long haul, and I went in with a determination that nothing and nobody would get in the way. I think that if you believe in something, to have the commitment is really more important than having the money.*

Ebony hit newsstands on November 1, 1945. Black readers scooped up the *Life*-sized publication, chock-full of articles and striking black-and-white photos chronicling black achievement: Jackie Robinson breaking the color barrier in baseball; Lena Horne dazzling thousands with her beauty and talent; A. G. Gaston building wealth and power as the most successful black businessman in the South. All of these milestones were celebrated on the pages of *Ebony*.

But Johnson's vision did not include glossing over the tough racial issues of the times. In his first editorial, Johnson wrote:

> Ebony *will try to mirror the happier side of Negro life—the positive everyday achievements from Harlem to Hollywood. But when we talk about race as the No. 1 problem in America, we'll talk turkey.*

Johnson set high standards for himself, announcing that he would not accept one page of advertising until he guaranteed a circulation of 100,000. With virtually no competition, the magazine surpassed its circulation goal in one year. The Audit Bureau of Circulation revealed that *Ebony*'s paid sales of more than 300,000 by the end of 1946 made it the most widely circulated black publication in the world.

But, in pushing *Ebony,* Johnson broke one of his cardinal rules: He grew too fast.

While *Negro Digest* was profitable, *Ebony* was draining the company's coffers. As a result, from 1945 to 1947, Johnson was forced to do everything he could to keep his fledgling company from sinking. He postponed the payment of bills, stalled creditors, and pounded the pavement in search of advertisers.

Ironically, *Ebony* became *too* successful. Its meager advertising base could not support the expense of printing and shipping 400,000 copies a month. It was a catch-22, though: If Johnson cut back on circulation, then he wouldn't be able to entice future advertisers. To make matters worse, local banks would still not loan him the funds for working capital because they wouldn't take a chance on a black businessman, despite his solid three-year track record.

For the first time in his life, Johnson was ready to throw in the towel.

> *I had serious doubts about whether I should go on. I would call my mother and tell her that I seemed to be failing. She would ask me, "Are you still trying?" I*

would tell her that I was. She would respond, "As long as you are trying then you are not a failure." Her words really pushed me. I was going to make sure that the business survived for her.

As he tried to cure his cash-flow crunch, he reminded himself that a businessman must always keep his options open. What if he could develop other businesses to generate additional revenues and support the magazine? With his network of distributors and a magazine that could promote products to thousands of black consumers, it could work. In fact, the crisis spawned Johnson's lifelong business strategy of using publications to promote his other business ventures.

I've never let the inability to get capital keep me from growing and surviving. I thought of all kinds of unique ways to survive. I sold lifetime subscriptions for $100 each. Since white advertisers would not advertise with Ebony, *I started a group of mail-order magazines and advertised in my own magazine. The company was called Beauty Star. I sold vitamins, wigs, dresses, and hair-care products. I sold anything that I could sell in order to get enough capital to keep* Ebony *going.*

But he couldn't sell enough subscriptions or novelty items to finance the publication long-term. However, the tactic bought him what he desperately needed—time. *Ebony*'s survival depended on bagging major advertisers. Johnson resolved to snare them, telling himself, "If I can't sell *Ebony* better than anyone else, I don't deserve to be president."

First, he needed to get the attention of major ad agencies. To reach top execs, he would woo the gatekeepers.

I cultivated secretaries. I would find out their birthday and send flowers to them. They appreciated my persistence and patience. This approach helped me when I tried to get a meeting with Fairfax Cone, the head of Foot, Cone & Belding advertising agency. His secretary said that she couldn't make an appointment for anyone but she grew to like me and gave me a valuable tip. She said, "Mr. Cone doesn't like to fly and goes to New York every Sunday afternoon on the Twentieth Century Limited. If I were you, I'd be on that train." I took her advice and for three consecutive Sundays, I traveled on the Twentieth Century Limited and managed to get an audience with him on those occasions. Shortly thereafter, he arranged for me to talk to executives at his agency.

In his presentations and editorials in *Ebony*, Johnson became the first publisher to discuss the power of the black consumer market. Unfortunately, it fell on deaf ears.

It was like trying to get them to put money in a foreign market.

He persisted, using his publication as a bully pulpit. In 1947, he wrote in *Ebony* that the "big advertisers of consumer items failed to recognize the immensity of the Negro market," more than $10 billion at the time. The response? Zero.

Finally, after yet another degrading sales call, he phoned advertising powerhouse Leo Burnett.

"Mr. Burnett, when I come to your company and talk to your representatives, they never listen to the pitches. They either shuffle papers or look out the window. All I want is five to ten minutes of their time."

"If they don't listen, I can't make them listen."

"I disagree," Johnson insisted. "They listen to you."

Burnett was persuaded to sit in the back of the room while Johson pitched his top execs. They listened, but still didn't bite. Johnson changed strategies again.

If he could penetrate the White House, he reassured himself, surely he could arrange a face-to-face meeting with CEOs of major companies. After all, it was plain corporate courtesy for one president to break bread with another.

Once an appointment was booked, he used guerrilla-style selling techniques, which called for him to learn as much detail as possible about the CEO he planned to pitch. He would uncover the concerns, desires, and idiosyncrasies of his intended target, and use them as tools to build a relationship. For instance, when he tried to sell advertising to Zenith, the leading manufacturer of radios, he learned that the head of the company, Commander Eugene McDonald, had explored the North Pole. Noting McDonald's obsession with polar expedition, Johnson tracked down Matthew Henson, the African American who beat Commodore Robert Peary to the Pole. He obtained Henson's inscription on a copy of his autobiography.

After receiving the book from Johnson as a gift, McDonald asserted, "Young man, if you were putting out any kind of magazine, you would have something on Matt Henson." As if on cue, Johnson pulled out an issue of *Ebony* that contained a four-page article on the explorer. In response, not only did McDonald place Zenith ads in *Ebony*, he proceeded to call the chairmen of such companies as the Armour Food Company, Swift Packing Company, and Elgin Watch Company—while Johnson sat in the room—and advised them to do the same.

Twenty-three years after that meeting with McDonald, Johnson was elected to Zenith's board of directors.

After two years of being on life support, *Ebony* and JPC were out of intensive care. In 1948, the magazine became profitable as it gained such major advertisers as PepsiCo, Colgate, Beechnut, and Seagram. While JPC strengthened its revenue base, Johnson increased his knowledge of the magazine publishing business. He even persuaded executives of Time Inc., the largest magazine publisher in the country, to teach him and his staff more about the advertising and circulation process.

Time Inc. sharing proprietary secrets? Sure, because they didn't consider *Ebony* or this black upstart to be competition. If they had only known. . . .

Lesson #4: Walk Around Anyone or Anything That Gets in Your Way

By the 1950s, before the age of 35, Johnson was a millionaire. As JPC rose to unprecedented heights, the naysayers ate their words. A moment Johnson relishes to this day came when Roy Wilkins, the NAACP official who originally pooh-poohed the concept of *Negro Digest,* called him and said, "You know, I think I gave you some bad advice."

Johnson had by now evolved into a more astute and confident businessman and publisher. Cast in *Ebony*'s glossy shadow, *Negro Digest* began to lose its luster—and money. Johnson realized that he needed to produce trendier magazines that were more in step with the times. He hated pulling the plug on the publication that started it all, but he refused to prop up any operation that would weaken JPC's bottom line.

Instead, Johnson acquired *Tan Confessions* and *Copper Romance* to satisfy the burgeoning romance magazine market. In 1950, he started *Hue,* a pocket-sized feature magazine, and, in 1951, the ever-popular *Jet,* which sold as many as 30,000 copies a week. At the same time, *Ebony*'s circulation soared to more than 500,000 copies.

Johnson no longer presided over a mom-and-pop business. He developed a stronger presence on Madison Avenue, setting up a New York–based advertising office. As usual, Johnson used every arrow in his quiver. To convince William P. Grayson, the ad director of the *Baltimore Afro-American,* to head up the New York sales office, Johnson hired him for more money than he paid himself and provided him with a more spacious office than his own Chicago suite. In later years, he would joke:

We gave him a big office. We paid him a big salary. We gave him a beautiful secretary. And then we threatened to take it all away from him. You'd be surprised how much we got out of him.

By 1955, the 13-year-old enterprise owned a stable of magazines with a combined circulation of 2.6 million and employed more than 100 professionals.

But the growth did not come without major challenges. Johnson and his employees constantly combatted racial discrimination. He adroitly maneuvered around such barriers. When Johnson traveled across the country selling ad space or identifying new distributors, he took along his circulation manager, a light-skinned man who could pass for white. The manager would register at hotels and then meet Johnson, who took the freight elevator, at the room. When Johnson bought his first building, an old mortuary south of Chicago's Loop, he hired a white lawyer to handle the transaction because the owner wouldn't sell it to a black man. It was bought in trust so no one could identify the buyer. Before the completion of the sale—the $50,000 down payment was derived from the sale of Beauty Star— Johnson disguised himself as a janitor to survey the property.

Johnson has no regrets about any of his tactics, maintaining that:

> *[JPC couldn't have made such strides] by marching, and we couldn't do it by threatening. We had to persuade people that it was in their best interests to reach out to black consumers in a positive way.*

Steadfastness would eventually win out over racism. In 1957, the entrepreneur started to branch out from his core business. Earl Dickerson, the attorney who gave him space and became CEO of Supreme Life after the death of Harry Pace, persuaded Johnson to buy shares in his former employer. He acquired 1000 shares in the company for $30,000 and joined its board of directors. Over the next 16 years, he pumped another $2.5 million into the operation and, by 1974, became chairman and CEO. Like in an old B movie, the office clerk made good and came back to take control of the company that launched his career.

But when he assumed the helm, he did things his way,

prompting some Supreme Life insiders to label him as arrogant and ruthless. Before Johnson took over, the insurer never fired employees, regularly transferring people from one department to another. He put the brakes on the practice, ousting anyone who couldn't cut it.

His next move to diversify the JPC empire was the 1958 launch of Ebony Fashion Fair. The traveling fashion show not only promoted the magazine and boosted circulation, but its events also raised millions of dollars for black charities. To this day, Ebony Fashion Fair remains an entertainment mainstay in many African American communities.

JPC grew in lockstep with the social movements of the 1960s. In words and pictures, *Ebony* and *Jet* chronicled the struggle of black Americans for advancement. From urban hubs to cotton fields, the magazines informed blacks about what was happening on the front lines of the Civil Rights Movement. With a new generation emerging, the publication took on a somewhat harder edge. Still criticized for its emphasis on celebrity profiles, society news, and positive articles—the old Johnson philosophy of getting consumers "to take castor oil by putting it in orange juice"—*Ebony* started devoting cover stories and whole issues to such provocative but relevant topics as "Black Power," "The White Problem in America," and "Black-on-Black Crime." The company launched a book division, filling the void in black history literature with Lerone Bennett's classic *Before the Mayflower*. Johnson also revived *Negro Digest* as *Black World*, his most militant publication, featuring radical pieces by black poets and fiction writers.

The aggressive editorial thrust was good business. By the mid-1960s, *Ebony* sold nearly a million copies a month and significantly broke the advertising barrier by grossing more than $5 million in advertising revenues—a vast difference from 20 years earlier when it earned less than $30,000 in advertising dollars. *Jet, Tan,* and *Black World* also boomed, with combined sales of 2.3 million copies a month.

But despite these strides, Johnson continued to be at

odds with the black press. Since the inception of *Ebony*, black newspaper publishers viewed him as a pirate, raiding readers, advertisers, and employees. Although the dissension bothered him, Johnson stayed true to form, making no apologies or excuses for doing things his way.

With the exception of John Sengstacke of the Chicago Defender, *I received a great deal of opposition from black newspapers. But we soon found that it didn't serve each other's purpose. On the recommendation of Sengstacke, I was voted in as a member of the Negro Newspaper Publishers Association at their Atlanta convention. Later, I was voted out of the organization saying the previous election violated the constitution. Finally, they accepted my application to the organization. These events did not ease the conflicts. In 1966, the NNPA honored me with the John Russwurm Award. Just before I received the award, the presenter told me, "Johnson, you deserve this award but I don't want you to misunderstand; we didn't like you before and we don't like you now."*

Being a pioneer has meant that Johnson has had to travel a solitary road. He accepted that reality early on. He came to thrive on it, even to prefer it. His hardscrabble youth as an only child gave him a great deal of time for inner reflection. Facing rejection and slights—much like Jackie Robinson, Jesse Owens, Sammy Davis, Jr., and other trailblazers—made him insular and understandably protective of his domain. Over the decades, he would buy, start, discontinue, and revive publications, but *Ebony* and *Jet* remained constant. They made everything else possible.

Johnson developed a diversified conglomerate as a means of sheltering JPC from economic downturns. For example, he launched Supreme Beauty Products to manufacture and distribute Duke and Raveen hair-care brands since orders came in for the old Beauty Star products even after he stopped running ads. Building on his franchise, he established radio stations WJPC in Chicago and WLOU in Louisville, Kentucky, and developed a series of television programs as well.

Other ventures Johnson launched purely out of frustration. In the 1960s, when Ebony Fashion Fair models had difficulty matching lipstick and makeup to their skin tones, Johnson went to Charles Revson, the legendary head of Revlon Cosmetics, and suggested that he consider expanding the line to accommodate women with darker complexions. Revson scoffed at the idea.

Perturbed, but characteristically unbowed, Johnson and his wife went to a private lab to develop an in-house line of cosmetics, which they eventually sold through JPC's mail-order operation. The response led to the 1973 creation of Fashion Fair Cosmetics. To sell the products, Johnson used the same tactic he developed 30 years earlier to get Chicago's largest distributor to carry *Negro Digest.*

When a buyer for Marshall Field's department store told Johnson that it never carried a cosmetics line for African Americans, *he didn't get mad, he got smart.* He soft-sold the buyer, telling him that Marshall Field's never found a black cosmetics line of the caliber of Fashion Fair. He hooked another fish.

Johnson's research revealed that successful beauty-care lines sold an average of $1200 a week. In order to convince the store that Fashion Fair was an instant hit, Johnson gave his employees money to buy $200 worth of the company's products a day. Based on those sales, Marshall Field's increased its order, and Johnson leveraged that success to get the line in major stores nationwide. Since Revlon and Estée Lauder did not have any black executives or salespeople, he trained newcomers to the business.

Fashion Fair became JPC's fastest-growing division when, ironically, it received patronage from not only black women but white women as well. England and France represent two of the company's top markets. Fashion Fair, which today accounts for roughly 50 percent of JPC's sales, competes directly with Revlon. Johnson once again has had the last laugh.

Lesson #5: You Can Grow It Alone

For 25 years, Johnson had been unable to convince potential investors and partners, black or white, to put money in any of his ventures. As a result, he stopped wanting any help. This go-it-alone philosophy seems anachronistic by today's models of success. Although he contends that "there are many ways to get to heaven"—meaning blacks should use any means available to them to advance in business—he takes exception to the swelling throng of black entrepreneurs who see strategic alliances with major companies as the only significant means for black companies to grow. Johnson holds that there is still room for black bootstrappers, even in a period marked by rampant mergers and acquisitions. It is imperative, he insists, that African American entrepreneurs preserve and control their businesses as a means of ensuring wealth and employment for black people.

That said, Johnson has not let his belief in control hamper his ability to recognize a valuable business opportunity. During the past 15 years, he has been a major investor in a Chicago cable franchise, and he bought a 20 percent stake in *Essence*, the black women's magazine, for roughly $1 million when it became available to him. ("Although I'm not seeking to acquire more, I would not refuse an offer to [let me] buy more," he says.) And, in 1994, Johnson broke his no-partners rule when he invested roughly $2.5 million to form EBCO International, teaming with five South African partners to develop *Ebony South Africa*. He did so to gain entrée into an untapped market and avoid stiff tariffs. When he started the venture, Johnson maintained a 51 percent share while his partners held 49 percent. By 1998, Johnson had increased his stake to 85 percent. He has no interest, however, in going public or merging with a mainstream monolith as it relates to the core of his empire, waving off calls from the investment community he attempted to court as a young man. In fact, he views the absence of partners in his core business as one of his greatest strengths.

For 10 years, I tried to get someone to joint venture with me to build a skyscraper in Chicago. I got a lot of inquiries, but as soon as they found out I was black, they remembered previous commitments. Nobody wanted to go in with me. I finally had to go it alone by saving money over a long period of time to build a small building that only my company could occupy. In hindsight, I believe that if I had partners, I would have never been as successful. It's difficult for a group of people to agree on one objective.

Lesson #6: Stay the Course

The 1970s to 1990s saw perhaps the most significant gains by African Americans in the educational and economic mainstream. Through coverage in his magazines and involvement in government bodies and corporate boards, Johnson played an instrumental role in that progression. At the same time, the razing of racial barriers has created major challenges for the House of Johnson.

Many of the leading beauty-care firms became converts to Johnson's gospel of the powerful black consumer market, but they saw more benefits in becoming competitors than advertisers. Majority newspapers and periodicals began hiring more African Americans and made attempts to raid his staff. Black white-collar and blue-collar workers got insurance through their jobs or mainstream firms that offered more sophisticated financial products.

The rapidly changing environment—albeit generally for the better—dealt the deathblow to traditional black businesses, among them Supreme Life, which Johnson was forced to sell in 1993. His infusion of millions into the company made it the fifth largest black-owned insurer in the nation. But like more than 20 other African American insurance firms, Supreme Life could not survive the industry-wide shakeout of the late 1980s and early 1990s. Johnson saw the handwriting on the wall for years but resisted the sale. He didn't want to put employees on the street. He didn't want to shut down an institution that gave him his start. Mostly, he didn't want to accept failure.

As for the hair care and cosmetics business, Johnson still employs "the Beauty Star concept." Reaching more than 50 percent of African American adults through his publications, he continues to promote his product lines in *Ebony* and *Jet*. In fact, JPC products still constitute about 20 percent of the company's own advertising pages.

As for *Ebony*, it continues to be criticized for its emphasis on celebrity profiles and puff pieces as opposed to more relevant, hard-hitting fare. The fact is, the light stuff sells. In 1997, the flagship—as well as *Jet*—had its best year ever in terms of the number of advertising pages sold. In 1998, 53-year-old *Ebony* got a face-lift that included brighter graphics, more service-oriented articles, and an infusion of content from its defunct sibling, *Ebony Man*. The retooling seems to be in response to the new crop of urban-oriented publications that have captured the hip youth market and other segments of the black community. Johnson remains steadfast in his mission to snag a fourth generation of African American reader.

As animated and forthright as he can be on many subjects, there are some things that John Johnson will not talk about. He will not divulge details about his succession scheme. Nor will he discuss his estate plan. He does say that his daughter, Linda, will take over the business, but gives no indication when that will happen.

For years, Linda Johnson Rice has been personally groomed by her father. As a child, she would come to the company and ask questions about all aspects of his business (a practice that has been adopted by her nine-year-old daughter Alexa, who meets with grandad every week to discuss the company's history). Linda earned her M.B.A. from Northwestern University while serving as assistant to the company president, a position requiring her to sit in on every important meeting, review her father's responses to correspondence, and take notes on how he made business decisions.

She has been the company's president and chief operating officer for more than a decade, but her mark is not yet apparent to the public. There is speculation that post–John Johnson, JPC would be sold. There is certainly no shortage of companies—black or white—that would love to buy it. But speculation is merely that.

For now, when one thinks about JPC, it is The Godfather who jumps to mind. That is not by coincidence, but by design. It is a direct response to Johnson's continuing to do business the Johnson way—no apologies or excuses required.

> *Linda will succeed me. Even now, I don't do anything that she doesn't agree on and she me. I call it a joint venture. But I am not going to retire anytime soon. I have a policy that as long as an employee is able to do the job, he or she can stay with the company. That includes me.*

2

ROBERT L. JOHNSON: BET HOLDINGS, INC.

The Brand Master

ROBERT L. JOHNSON

Age: 53.

Birthplace: Freeport, Illinois.

Marital Status: Married 30 years to Sheila Crump Johnson, BET's executive vice president of corporate affairs and a member of the board of directors.

Children: A daughter, Paige, 13; a son, Brett, 9.

Education: University of Illinois, B.S., political science; Princeton University, M.P.A.

Entity: BET Holdings, Inc.

Established: 1980.

Corporate Headquarters: Washington, D.C.

Products: Black Entertainment Television cable network; BET On Jazz: The Cable Jazz Channel; BET Movies/STARZ³ channel; BET Action Pay-Per-View; *Emerge* magazine; *BET Weekend* magazine; *Heart & Soul* magazine; Arabesque Books; MSBET on-line service; BET Soundstage theme restaurants in Largo, Maryland, and BET Soundstage Club in Orlando, Florida; BET On Jazz restaurant; EXSTO XXIV VII men's clothing line; and BET Financial Services (Visa card sponsored by Chevy Chase Bank in Maryland).

Annual Sales: $170 million.

Number of Employees: 563.

Corporate Mission: To establish BET as the preeminent brand of choice among black consumers.

First Job: Managing an unsuccessful newspaper route.

First Career Move: Public affairs director for the Corporation for Public Broadcasting.

Role Model: John C. Malone, president and CEO of Tele-Communications, Inc. (TCI), aka "The Cable King."

On Networking: *All business is personal. . . . Make your friends before you need them.*

2

ROBERT L. JOHNSON:
BET HOLDINGS, INC.

The Brand Master

W e look for strategic partners that can bring something to
the equation. I believe that two plus two should equal five.

In October 1991 Bob Johnson made history.

After dealing with years of resistance from investment
banks, analysts, portfolio managers, and institutional
moneymen, the smooth, young entrepreneur accomplished what scores of black-owned companies had tried
but couldn't pull off. Even the late Reginald F. Lewis, the
legendary CEO of TLC Beatrice International Holdings,
Inc., and architect of the only black-owned billion-dollar-
plus corporation in the world, failed in his attempt.

Not only did Johnson take his 11-year-old BET Holdings, Inc., public, but he placed it on the Big Board. For
the first time ever, a company owned and controlled by
African Americans was traded on the New York Stock Exchange. BET Holdings, parent of the Black Entertainment
Television cable channel, was up there alongside such
American institutions as IBM and AT&T.

The network of wealthy African American professionals
and business owners anticipated the Homeric event. Some
made a small fortune on the purchase and quick sale of
their shares. Others held on to the stock as a long-term
investment—and a powerful symbol of black capitalism.

The months of coast-to-coast road shows and meetings
with lawyers, accountants, and investment bankers paid

off. BET offered 4.25 million shares of stock at $17 a share. The stock shot up as investors bid as high as $26.37 a share. Johnson's foresight, pluck, and nerve yielded $72.3 million for his company, and $6.4 million personally when he sold 375,000 of his own 4.5 million shares.

Flush with cash, Johnson pushed on to his ultimate goal: creating the most recognized black-oriented brand on Earth. Now a member of a very exclusive club, he was determined that nothing would stop him.

The love affair lasted less than three months.

In mid-December, Johnson received a series of alarming calls from analysts. They asked him why a darling of Wall Street several weeks ago was turning into a flea-bitten dog.

A December 16 conference call with analysts went like this:

"Is BET's viewership eroding?" asked one.

"Of course not," replied Johnson.

"Then why did BET report that the network is reaching only 27.5 million homes when at the time the stock was offered, A. C. Nielsen [the television audience research firm] counted 31.6 million last summer?"

"BET only counted homes that paid for our service. Nielsen counted everyone who received it. They even counted viewers who were getting the service as part of a free trial promotion."

Good enough answer, but they weren't convinced. The Street smelled blood.

Over the next few days, several institutional investors bailed out and BET shares dropped like a ton of bricks. The stock price plummeted a staggering 56 percent to $15 a share—lower than its offering price.

Johnson got his first brutal lesson as CEO of a publicly traded company. When he ran BET as a private concern, he answered to a few select partners, his bankers, and the taxman. Now, he had to satisfy legions of shareholders. The Street appreciated only earnings and growth. If a company stumbled, loyalty be damned.

Johnson's public composure concealed the dismay of

seeing his company's market value going straight down the tubes. Now, more than ever, he had to maintain his aura of control. Never one to pause at the gate, Johnson moved quickly to extinguish the fire. To bolster shareholder confidence, he instructed his public relations staff to set up interviews and send out press releases to the financial press and general media reinforcing the message that BET's audience was growing at a spectacular clip, which was true, and that the subscriber data had been misinterpreted.

Then he worked the phones. Johnson called major shareholders, such as his mentor, John C. Malone, the president of Tele-Communications, Inc., and one of the most powerful men in cable, as well as portfolio managers like top media investor Mario Gabelli. His case: BET had survived and expanded over the past decade while larger, well-heeled networks had not seen a cent of profit. The network reached people on more than 2400 cable systems, and no other network was better positioned to seize viewers as urban America was being wired. In 1990, the company grossed $50.8 million, up an astonishing 41 percent from the previous year, and sales would continue to surge in the future. Cash flow and net income had risen by 88 percent and 77 percent, respectively.

The straight talk worked. Within a month, the stock rebounded to $25 a share.

> *BET was new to the marketplace and, initially, we were inexperienced in answering the kinds of questions that the analysts asked. It was a tough period for us. Once that was resolved, the IPO [initial public offering] eventually worked out great for us. We were able to get the money that we needed to make strategic business decisions and it gave us the ability to raise as much as $100 million. The value of going public for any company is access to expansion capital. For one, you can use your stock as collateral to borrow money. I am proud that we became a black company that broke a barrier. The offering was the first step in positioning BET as an enterprise worth $1 billion.*

Wired for Success

It's June 1998 in Orlando, Florida. The oppressive night heat doesn't stop a sea of African American tourists from crowding in front of a platform at Pleasure Island, Disney World's wonderland for grown-ups. BET is about to announce yet another venture. Since the IPO, it seems as if the media conglomerate had been doing deals by the hour.

Casually attired, the man who would be king of cable takes center stage as his audience enthusiastically greets him with applause and palms pumping into the air.

He is the star of the moment, here to unveil the BET Soundstage Club, the second such outlet he has opened in two years. Adopting the tactic popularized by Planet Hollywood and the Hard Rock Cafe, Johnson plans to roll out a score of these nightspots over the next five years and then spin the chain off in a public offering.

Johnson is typically low-key, but tonight his excitement shows. Years back, he vowed that BET would "have the same perception in the black community that Disney has in the general community." So, it's almost poetic that his establishment is the first black theme restaurant ever to grace the Magic Kingdom. The project signals an alliance between one of the world's communications giants and the preeminent black entertainment company. "We are honored to be a part of history. . . . This partnership represents a great marriage of brands."

History, partnerships, brands. These are the things of which Bob Johnson's dreams are made. Every deal he consummates or venture he undertakes moves forward his grand scheme to expand an "umbrella brand" that shelters a diverse array of black-oriented enterprises. BET's black-and-gold star logo appears on four cable channels, where its viewers watch videos, films, and news programs; a Web site developed with Microsoft, where subscribers download information on black entertainment; a Visa card, which customers can use to pay for BET-related leisure activities and anything else their hearts desire; a branded clothing line; a stable of publications led by an entertainment magazine with a readership of 1.2 million; and a proposed casino-hotel in Las Vegas.

To construct such a dynamic entertainment complex, Johnson shrewdly crafts strategic partnerships, teaming only with corporations that bring in large amounts of capital and expertise. Using the BET brand as a fulcrum, he often leaves the negotiating table holding the majority ownership stake or lead management role.

At 53, the trim, polished CEO presides over a $170 million empire by tapping seemingly unlimited reserves of energy. He thrives on continuous stimuli, completing complex transactions while managing a whirlwind schedule. One day before lunch, he finished a conference call about developing a gaming operation in the Caribbean, met with business partners about producing a series of jazz concerts, reviewed the company's new Canadian operations, and discussed ideas for a magazine joint venture. Every moment of every day his concern is about getting things done. No wonder his assistant guards his schedule like a bulldog.

Johnson, a dashing figure in tailored suits and expressive ties who speaks in a slow, measured manner but can loosen audiences up with jokes, feels he can't afford to waste time. He has tremendous focus and a rare—and valuable—ability not to dwell on success or failure. On a flight back to Washington, Debra Lee, his president and chief operating officer (COO), beams over a $10 million deal they have just put to bed. Johnson listens for a couple of minutes and then asks, "What's next?"

Admittedly—and ironically—Johnson is not a big fan of television, tuning in only to news, an occasional football game, and, of course, his own programming. But he maintains a healthy respect for the tube's power. He used it to come into millions of African American homes with music videos, lame sitcom reruns, jazz performances, public affairs shows, and infomercials. It's the machine that sells ads, promotes products, and influences the political process. It has fed all of his interests—business, entertainment, politics—and produced for him a net worth in excess of $100 million, making him one of richest African Americans in the nation.

In the past, he has boasted about his company being professionally managed, run minus the candy-store mentality or force of personality emblematic of most black companies started by iron-willed entrepreneurs. Part of the reason is that some of his employees have owned company stock, so their wealth is tied into BET's corporate performance. He ensures that the managers understand BET's overall strategic thrust and lets his team, a mix of veterans and employees he has snatched up from ESPN, the New York Times Company, Time Warner, and the like, run with the ball. His eight-member board of directors is composed of six outsiders, himself, and his wife, Sheila, who is BET's executive vice president of corporate affairs.

> *I want to create an institutionalized view of black business that has nothing to do with the individual CEO but [with] business strategies and objectives. Our company tends to be in perpetual motion. We believe in being very aggressive with our acquisitions and joint ventures so that we can develop unique brands under the BET umbrella. We believe in developing deals with major companies because the transactions bring a capital structure and management insularity. We look for strategic partners that can bring something to the equation. I believe that two plus two should equal five.*

While Johnson's corporate vision may not be ego-driven, his success has earned him a heady slot among the nation's business and political elite. President Clinton included him on his trade mission to Africa in April 1998. He also is one of the few entrepreneurs, white or black, to receive an invitation to investment banker Herb Allen's exclusive Sun Valley, Idaho, retreat for the nation's most powerful communications barons. In addition to his partners, Malone and Bill Gates of Microsoft, Johnson hobnobs with CNN's Ted Turner, News Corporation's Rupert Murdoch, and Universal Studios' Edgar Bronfman, Jr. Such power networking will inevitably lead to other synergistic deals.

Not bad for a poor kid from the Midwest.

Robert Louis Johnson grew up in the small hamlet of Freeport, Illinois during the 1950s and 1960s. A child of television, he favored cowboy heroes in such programs as *Hopalong Cassidy, Cisco Kid,* and *Gunsmoke.* At the age of nine, he got his first taste of business by managing an unsuccessful newspaper route. As a teenager, he wanted to be a fighter pilot. Less than perfect sight prevented him from pursuing that dream. But whenever presented with failure in life or business, Johnson simply looks for another endeavor in which to sink his teeth. When Sheila Johnson is asked what drives her husband, she states: "He's number nine of ten children. He grew up not having much." In short, she says, "He's hungry."

He graduated from the University of Illinois with a degree in political science. His good grades and an interest in foreign matters gained him admittance into the prestigious Woodrow Wilson School of Public and International Affairs at Princeton University, where he earned a master's degree in public administration. Then, it was off to Washington, D.C., where he worked briefly as public affairs director for the Corporation for Public Broadcasting and director of communications for the local branch of the Urban League. In 1973, at 26, he was hired as press secretary for District of Columbia Representative Walter Fauntleroy. Three years later, it was time for a change.

At a neighbor's party, Johnson learned about an opening at the National Cable Television Association (NCTA), a trade group representing more than 1500 cable television companies. In 1976, cable TV was in its infancy and Johnson was seeking new challenges. Maybe, he thought, this was an industry where he would finally be able to soar.

As NCTA's vice president of pay television and, later, vice president for government relations, Johnson was one of the industry's chief lobbyists. He had learned well how to schmooze and get things done as a congressional flack. Now he would solicit and build relationships with cable's emerging powers and take his deal-cutting skills to a new level.

I think the biggest lesson I learned during those years is that all business is personal. I found that many times the business facts would not argue for a relationship to exist but the personal relationship and personal rapport override it. I remember Bob Smith, the head of the NCTA, telling me: "Make your friends before you need them." That basic advice has served me well throughout the years.

In fact, if there has been a single key to Johnson's success, it has been his ability to cultivate friendships with powerful men. In politics and business, his efficiency, energy, organizational skill, and charm draw people to him like a magnet. Once there, Johnson makes sure they stick.

He wasn't a drive-by friend, calling people only when he needed them. As part of his daily routine, he scheduled calls to check up on associates. Before his mogul days, he was extremely generous with his time and freely provided favors and support. In 1978, for instance, he helped a local civil rights activist named Marion Barry, Jr., become mayor of the nation's capital. He vigorously campaigned for Barry and coached him on how to project an image of trust and confidence. In the process, he developed a friendship and unconstrained access to city hall. Within the span of a decade, Johnson managed to fill his Rolodex with influential insiders from Capitol Hill, the cable industry, and local government.

By 1979, cable television had started moving beyond rural and suburban communities. New companies began developing programming for different segments of the population, spawning such networks as MTV and CNN. People who had been close to the industry, like NCTA staffers, were trying to figure out how they could cash in on the boom. The concept for BET grew out of a discussion that Johnson had with a colleague about a new cable channel for senior citizens.

"Senior citizens watch a lot of television. Many of them feel that they're not properly treated in the medium," his colleague said. "They represent a significant amount of buying power, and advertisers would probably be interested in reaching that audience."

Johnson replied, "You know, the same thing can be said about black Americans."

He requested a copy of his colleague's notes and changed all of the references from elderly to black. That document formed the framework for a cable network targeted at African Americans. He conducted additional research and developed a business plan. Next was the crucial goal: financing.

To get the ball rolling, he secured a $15,000 personal loan from the National Bank of Washington. But he needed bigger—much bigger—bucks if he was serious about launching a full-fledged television network.

Looking for sources of capital, he scanned his Rolodex and came across the name of John C. Malone. An electrical engineer by training, Malone rose to become one of the most powerful men in cable, controlling Tele-Communications, Inc. (TCI), the mammoth cable operation plugged into more than 10 million homes.

Malone was interested in diversified programming to feed his sprawling complex of cable systems. He also respected Johnson's reputation as an effective lobbyist for the industry and believed the 33-year-old had the right stuff to develop such a network. Furthermore, he realized that if the channel became successful, he could use it to capture emerging urban franchises.

The two met at TCI's company headquarters in Denver. The budding entrepreneur and the cable magnate sat across the table from one another.

"How much do you need?" Malone asked.

"A half million dollars."

"Tell you what I'll do," Malone said. "I'll buy into your network for $180,000 and I'll loan you $320,000."

"Fine. How much do you want?"

"I want twenty percent of the company."

"That's all you want?"

"Yeah. That's all."

"Deal."

Even Johnson was stunned by the speed and ease of one of the most important transactions of his life.

"I have one word of advice, though," Malone offered.

"What's that?"

"Keep your revenues up and your costs down."

Malone backed Johnson in part, he says, because "Bob seemed like the kind of guy that you could invest some money with, and he wouldn't embarrass you. When we thought about starting this, there was always the concern that this kind of a channel could become radical, and you wouldn't want your name associated with it."

Nobody helped Johnson more than Malone. Over the years, his mentor showed him the ropes, gave his network credibility, acted as a sounding board for new ideas, introduced him to media heavyweights, invested in his other businesses through TCI's Liberty Media Corporation and Encore Media subsidiaries, and extended invitations—business and social—that would enable Johnson to grow his company as well as his own coffers.

> *I have to admit that there was a bit of luck involved in starting BET. I came as the industry was expanding. I was fortunate that John Malone was such a visionary. BET got started because he made the decision to embrace diversity. That was a time when few believed that there was a need for a channel targeted to black consumers. BET was the first programming service that John Malone invested in. He served as my mentor in the cable business. When he joined the board, he added prestige to our company.*

With his modest relative investment, Johnson was ready to start. In January 1980, just six months after being formed, BET went into operation, reaching a meager 3.8 million households. For programming, he acquired the rights to black-oriented films from United Artists such as *Lady Sings the Blues* and *Willie Dynamite*. He managed to gain four hours of satellite time, 11 P.M. to 3 A.M., on Friday nights. BET was up on its feet and taking baby steps forward. But there was nothing infantile about Johnson's vision.

At the opening reception of BET, he read from the memoirs of CBS patriarch William S. Paley. Brimming with confidence, Johnson maintained that his upstart network would break even within three years. He spoke enthusiastically and, many thought, naively: "I want to be a communications giant."

Phases of Growth

Johnson advises novice entrepreneurs that business ventures will be marked by three distinct phases of evolution. The trick is being scrappy and resourceful enough to reach each plateau.

> *BET, like most entrepreneurial operations that start from scratch and last for a number of years, went through three stages of development. In the first phase, I didn't have much staff, so I literally had to do just about everything myself. There was very little distinction between the lines of management. In the second phase, I was managing a small group of people but I still had to be extremely hands-on. I supported them on an individualized basis and provided them with resources. By the third phase, I was able to develop a sophisticated management team that could follow my strategic vision for the company. They are accountable for meeting specific goals and timetables.*

Launched on a shoestring budget, BET was continually strapped for cash. Johnson expanded at a deliberate pace, recruiting young and inexperienced professionals who learned their jobs as he was trying to figure out his role as CEO. He personally handled much of the heavy lifting—generating revenues and managing cash flow.

Back then, BET made its money from two streams: advertising and fees from cable operators that carried the service. But to advertisers and cable systems, a network that aired four hours weekly had little appeal and virtually no clout. Consequently, he operated a company so lean that industry analysts were making wagers on when BET would go bust.

> *My toughest challenge was trying to get advertisers. They wanted to see Nielsen ratings before committing to ad dollars. We didn't have a big enough audience to earn any ratings. During sales pitches, advertisers would tell me, "Blacks don't subscribe to cable." To make matters worse, a lot of operators wouldn't take us. It was a tough sell. There were times I didn't think we were going to make it.*

In true Johnson fashion, he simply kept on keeping on. There was no way the network could stay afloat if he waited on the payment cycle of 30 days or more from advertisers and cable operators. Most sponsors didn't pay for spots until three months after they agreed to place an ad, cutting a check after they received affidavits that their commercial was broadcast.

So Johnson lobbied them. He came to realize that textbook tactics wouldn't cut it. He had to beg, plead, promise, and pray to preserve his network. He tried to convince them to make special financing arrangements based on the fact that BET was a hand-to-mouth operation. He made the rounds of advertisers, cable operators, and programming suppliers, asking for "front-end support."

When he pitched Anheuser-Busch, Johnson was mindful of the fact that the maker of Budweiser beer regularly advertised in African American publications and on black radio. So he was hopeful as he explained to its ad rep about the channel's potential, the growth of urban cable markets, and the advantages of being on the ground floor of the next big thing. But key to his presentation was the fact that he needed bucks up front. He minced no words in closing his appeal: "BET is a struggling company. Give us a break. Grow with us."

The rep acquiesced, but on his own terms, pointing out, "We need your advertising but not as bad as you need our money." Johnson couldn't much argue with that.

Advertisers like Anheuser-Busch, those that earned millions from selling products to black consumers, agreed to pay in advance in exchange for a flat rate over four years based on potential subscribers.

But the cable operators didn't give an inch. On average, the network received 2.5 cents per household, among the lowest fees of any programming service. Many operators flatly refused to carry the channel because they believed it didn't have enough capacity. Johnson could only hope that the systems would grow as more people became attracted to their programming and, in turn, BET would automatically grow, too.

In August 1982, the network started transmitting for six hours daily with a programming mix driven primarily by music videos and taped black college sports. The goal of Jeffri Lee, the then 25-year-old vice president of network operations, was to keep the extended format operational for 100 days. That's what it would take, Johnson believed, for BET to gain the confidence of operators and advertisers. Lee struggled to maintain the schedule, not sure whether it would exceed the company's technological capabilities. But he pulled it off.

When he phoned his boss bursting with news of his achievement, the response was vintage Johnson: "Good. . . . Just keep it going."

Johnson was already focused on lining up new investors. With TCI's help, he persuaded Taft Broadcasting, one of the nation's largest program syndicators, to purchase a 20 percent equity interest in BET for $1 million. Taft's clout enabled BET to acquire new shows at reasonable prices.

A turning point came in 1984. That year, he convinced HBO, a subsidiary of Time Inc. (now Time Warner, Inc.), to become a shareholder. HBO purchased shares from Johnson, TCI, and Taft. The new ownership configuration gave Johnson 52 percent of the stock and the other three partners 16 percent each. The total investment came to $6 million.

The new arrangement also insulated Johnson from potential competitors. From the beginning, he was concerned that other media companies would try to muscle into his territory. By snaring the largest players in cable distribution and programming as partners, Johnson quashed any new challengers that may have arisen.

That same year, BET gained 7.6 million subscribers and began transmitting 24 hours a day—even though it did not have enough programming. Johnson found a way to fill airtime and generate cash by leasing time to companies that produced infomercials offering everything from hair-care supplies to exercise equipment. The strategy didn't dazzle viewers or garner ratings, but it kept the screen from fading to black. Fact was, Johnson had no choice. He knew that the weight of additional overhead costs would crush his operation if he tried to develop original programming at this stage in the game.

While building his network and holding lengthy conversations with Malone, Johnson realized he needed to grab the reins of distribution in order to increase market share. So he invested $100,000 to form District Cablevision, Inc. (DCI), an operator that bid on the D.C. cable franchise. As the outfit's president, he parlayed his business and political connections into winning the bid to wire the city. Afterward, he disclosed that DCI had difficulty in raising the $50 million needed to build the system. Malone stepped in and became DCI's banker, providing the entire cost of initial construction. Through a limited partnership, the cable giant eventually took a 75 percent ownership stake in the operation. Since minority input and influence was a city council mandate for awarding the franchise, Malone's initial investment in BET and relationship with Johnson helped assuage the city fathers.

Meanwhile, Johnson was still struggling to augment distribution and programming for the network. To survive until his subscriber base grew large enough to generate ratings and attract advertisers, Johnson had borrowed as much as $10 million from his three equity partners. BET was growing, but its insatiable appetite for capital was eating away at Johnson's controlling interest. Despite this, his determination was unbowed.

He knew that if he could just convince advertisers to purchase more airtime, persuade his partners to restructure debt, and get employees to continue to work long, god-awful hours, then BET would be vindicated by the inevitable shift in the industry. In 1986, his prayers were answered. Large cities like Washington, Baltimore, and New York completed the wiring of their systems as black consumers pumped $500 million into the cable business. The network's subscribers reached 12 million, and finally showed up on the Nielsen meter.

Finally, BET was in the black.

Validated at last, Johnson sent dollar bills encased in Lucite to his top managers to mark the occasion. The staff, many still newcomers to television, grew to 40 people.

In 1989, BET Holdings earned $4 million in operating cash flow on $23 million in revenues. Despite the turnaround, he continued his practice of getting programming on the cheap: 16 hours each day were devoted to music videos, which the network received from record companies free of charge, and he convinced the Directors Guild of America to grant BET a waiver of the residuals on sitcoms no longer aired on television networks. The result of his penny-pinching? A sleek-tiled, $10 million production facility in northeast Washington.

Johnson was gearing up for Phase Three.

He would develop an enterprise that would dominate black entertainment, including nightclubs, apparel, and licensed products—BET's exclusive domain.

Now all he needed was cash, and the amount he sought could be found in only one place: the public markets.

Johnson Rule #1: Find the Capital You Need to Grow

BET's IPO turned out to be an example of how companies, especially black-owned enterprises, could gain access to expansion capital. For one, BET was an undisputed leader in a growing industry. Second, BET had developed a solid track record for being financially sound, regularly making its debt payments and paying its employees. The concern remained: Would it be able to stand up to the due diligence process as investment bankers, lawyers, accountants, analysts, and portfolio managers reviewed all of the company's audited financial statements and investigated legal skirmishes to see if it has been sued by creditors, vendors, or customers? BET, like any company going public, was bound by law to share such information with institutional and individual investors. And, even though it had a brilliant legal mind and proven deal maker in Debra Lee, the company's general counsel at the time, Johnson brought in a phalanx of experienced legal and financial advisers who knew the intricacies and pitfalls of such an offering.

To maintain control, Johnson instructed his investment bankers to issue two classes of stock—nonvoting common stock and stock with voting rights that could not be traded in the public market. Bear Stearns in Los Angeles and First Boston Corporation underwrote the sale of 21 percent of BET stock. Johnson thought it would sell at between $11 and $13. Wall Street was amazed when the stock, which was offered at $17, was oversubscribed by a whopping 54 million shares.

Taft, which had been gobbled up by Great American Entertainment Corporation, cashed out its entire 2.4 million shares. BET sold 1.5 million shares for $23 million. At the time, Johnson's publicly traded shares were worth $104.5 million while he retained 4.8 million Class C shares that gave him control of 56 percent of the company. TCI still owned 18 percent while Time Warner owned 15 percent (in 1995, Time Warner sold its shares for $50 million).

One unique aspect of the BET offering was implemented by Lemuel Daniels, a vice president of Bear Stearns, who marketed the shares specifically to the African American community, a practice that had never been executed by a Wall Street firm. Based in Los Angeles, Daniels knew the wealthiest African Americans in business and entertainment. Many influential blacks remembered how financier Reginald Lewis had been rebuffed when he tried to take TLC Beatrice public as analysts and mainstream financial journalists poked and prodded until the transaction became unhinged. They were determined that it would not happen again. African Americans—from B.E. 100s CEOs to corporate professionals—rallied behind the transaction.

A company that had a capitalization of $500,000 in 1980 had a capitalization of $325 million by 1991. It was unbelievable. One of the things that was significant about the offering was to see the wealth creation among African Americans. The IPO helped make black millionaires and enable others to generate ownership through equities. One of the most important things that I was able to do was enrich some of the people who helped to build the company. That is something that makes me extremely proud. I hope it serves as a model for other black businesses.

Johnson was now head of a public company and, as such, had to be careful when describing different aspects of the business. A sharp drop in earnings or viewership, as had been indicated in December 1991, could mean that the market value would plunge. Conversely, BET couldn't have too much free cash flow. If it were not reinvested or paid out as dividends, then it communicated that the company was stagnant.

Johnson Rule #2: Create Strategic Partnerships

Now deep into Phase Three, Johnson serves as a true chairman, shaping the company's long-term strategy. No more selling ads or begging creditors to restructure payment terms. His senior management team, which includes high-powered attorneys and executives lured from rival cable networks and media companies, carries out the day-to-day activities. But the transition from hands-on management did not go off without a hitch. In October 1992, he had to fire BET's chief financial officer and comptroller for embezzling $700,000 of corporate funds.

By 1998, roughly 90 percent of company revenues came from its core cable business, which includes the BET Cable Network, BET On Jazz, and BET Action Pay-Per-View. Johnson would like to see the cable operations produce 60 percent of gross sales while ancillary businesses—magazine publishing, restaurants, apparel, and the like—comprise the remaining 40 percent.

As in his past dealings, he still relies on strategic partnerships to advance the franchise. Part of Johnson's mastery in finding the right partnerships is his intimate knowledge of his customer base. When he acquired Action Pay-Per-View, he knew that such programming was heavily used by African Americans and Latinos for sporting events and movies. As avid fans of action movies, he figured he could reach another 7 million homes. In 1997, BET and Liberty Media Corporation, which owns Encore Media, developed BET Movies/Starz 3, a black movie channel. BET will contribute $24 million over three years to the network but benefits from access to the company's massive library of current Hollywood films.

Despite this continued reliance on growth through partnership, his philosophy holds that such relationships must add value and help catapult BET to reach its long-range goals. His method for assessing this is cut-and-dried. He thumbs down transactions that don't pay for themselves by either providing access to new conduits of distribution and capital, expanding lines of products and services, or fueling brand promotion. Take his ambitious strategy to develop the $200 million BET Soundstage-themed Casino in Las Vegas. As a board member of Hilton Hotels Corporation, he convinced the hotelier that a BET establishment would best attract the 2.5 million African American consumers who visit the city each year. Awarded a casino license in 1997, BET will supply the entertainment and marketing side of the venture while Hilton manages the hotel and gaming.

Although some partners have changed, TCI, which now

owns 22 percent of BET stock through its subsidiary, Liberty Media Corporation, has been the most consistent player. In fact, Malone has not sold one share of BET since his fateful first meeting with Johnson close to 20 years ago.

Going Private

Going public made all of the acquisitions and joint ventures possible, but it has proven to be an annoying obstacle as well. In 1996, Johnson discontinued the award-winning *Young Sisters and Brothers (YSB)* magazine, a five-year-old teen publication that was losing about $1.5 million a year, largely because shareholders believed that it was taking too long to turn a profit.

> *When a company goes public, an entrepreneur has to realize that his primary objective is to create shareholder value. You have to be very clear in communicating the strategic vision of your company. Some individual and institutional shareholders didn't understand our objective. They would ask, "Why are you in magazine publishing or clothing apparel? You're a cable company." You have to decide when staying public gets in the way of growth.*

In October 1997, Johnson decided that it was time to buy out the 6 million publicly traded shares. He had grown weary of the pressure to show rising profits and a higher stock price each quarter. He and Liberty Media offered shareholders $48 a share for the outstanding shares, a deal that valued BET at almost $800 million. At the time, news of the buyout pushed shares to $52.

The offer immediately pitted Johnson against some of BET's shareholders. Many claimed that the entrepreneur was trying to buy the company stock on the cheap. Dissidents believed that BET was worth almost 50 percent more. High-profile fund manager Mario Gabelli said that BET "is such a fabulous company that I see Johnson's offer as nothing more than preliminary," and pushed the company to increase its bid. The offer drew five lawsuits against Johnson, Malone, and the board of directors, which includes movie star Denzel Washington and National Public Radio president Delano Lewis.

In late January 1998, the special independent committee of the board, consisting of only Lewis, determined that the buyback "was not adequate." In March, Johnson sweetened his bid to $63 a share, which the board approved.

Despite the legal wrangling, Johnson achieved his goal. By July, the higher bid pushed BET's market value to $1.2 billion, with Johnson owning 63 percent, Liberty Media 35 percent, and Debra Lee 2 percent.

As the company grows fiscally stronger, its audience has become more demanding. Why, they ask, doesn't BET have more original programming? The short answer, of course, is that it's too expensive. Johnson's spin, as put to a recent conference of black professionals, is far less direct:

> *Videos are why we're where we are today. We're definitely committed to the music video. It will be the hallmark of BET.*

That's not to say that BET hasn't broken some ground. The network has held provocative and informative town meetings on topics including affirmative action and racial tolerance. It was the first network to land a televised interview with O. J. Simpson following his acquittal. (The interviewer, Ed Gordon, was immediately snatched up by MSNBC.)

As cable operators reduce the amount that they pay for basic cable—BET will receive about 14 cents per subscriber per month—programming will have to be bolstered in order to expand viewership and, in turn, advertising revenues. Part of Johnson's strategy calls for developing programs that do triple duty—add viewers, increase sponsorship, and promote new ventures. In fall 1998, he launched a prime-time nightly concert series, *BET Soundstage,* where the latest artists perform at his restaurant/nightclub, and *Heart & Soul*, a health and fitness show based on the publication that he purchased from Rodale Press.

After attending the 1998 Sun Valley conference of the nation's top communications magnates, Johnson revealed that he plans to develop a film studio to produce movies targeted for the black middle class. Clinging to his tightwad ways, he seeks to make low-budget films that will cost $3 million to $5 million each and release them in theaters in 25 major urban centers. The motion pictures, in turn, will be used as programming for his cable networks.

If you assume that black Americans' entertainment and leisure-time consumption is in the neighborhood of $20 billion, it would be as large as the cable industry by itself. For BET to seek control of a $20 billion market doesn't give me a whole lot of time to worry about anything else. And I don't mind not worrying about that so-called potential crossover market. I want to be in a position one day where, if Ebony magazine was being sold, or some other black media brands were on the block, BET would be the buyer of choice. I want BET to be the financier of choice for the young, black entrepreneurs with creative ideas about programming or information or entertainment. We're looking at any business that targets that marketplace and makes sense.

Next stop: Phase Four.

3

CLARENCE O. SMITH:
ESSENCE COMMUNICATIONS, INC.

The Salesman

CLARENCE O. SMITH

Age: 65.

Birthplace: Bronx, New York.

Marital Status: Married to wife, Elaine, for 35 years.

Children: Two sons, Clarence, Jr. (Lance), 31, and Craig, 26.

Education: City College of New York.

Entity: Essence Communications, Inc.

Established: 1969.

Corporate Headquarters: New York, New York.

Products: *Essence* magazine; *Latina* magazine; *Income Opportunities* magazine; Essence Entertainment; Essence Music Festival; Essence Awards television program; Essence by Mail; and Essence children's books.

Annual Sales: $104.8 million.

Mission: To make *Essence* a diversified brand synonymous with African American womanhood.

Number of Employees: 136.

First Professional Job: Freight forwarder for a customs agency.

Heroes: A. G. Gaston, named *Black Enterprise* Entrepreneur of the Century in 1992; Herman J. Russell, president and CEO of H. J. Russell & Company; John H. Johnson, publisher of *Ebony* magazine; and William Hudgins and baseball legend Jackie Robinson, founders of Freedom National Bank, the first black-owned bank in New York City.

Smith's Basics: *Plan your work and be willing to make adjustments. Raise enough money for a cushion. Respect the competition and assume that they are smarter than you.*

On Partnerships: *Regardless of what my partners did, I made a commitment that I would do everything in my power to make the magazine a success.*

On Ambition: *Doing well and doing good are absolutely not mutually exclusive.*

On the Innocence of Youth: *We thought that the world was waiting for this idea and that if we could just get the magazine out, advertisers would flock to it and black women would buy it. We had no idea how difficult it would be.*

3

CLARENCE O. SMITH: ESSENCE COMMUNICATIONS, INC.

The Salesman

Selling is not about conning someone out of something. . . . Sales is a value exchange . . . the goods or services are worth more to him than the money he is taking out of his pocket.

Clarence Smith had hit a dry spell.

For a year, he had been pounding the pavement, trying to push companies to buy ads in *Essence* magazine, the black women's publication that he founded with his three partners—Edward Lewis, Cecil Hollingsworth, and Johnathan Blount—in 1969.

As usual, he had done his homework, spending 18 months studying the competition and the advertising that filled their glossy pages. Estée Lauder. Revlon. Chanel. Pond's cold cream. None of them had ever made an appeal to black women. It was virgin territory.

Erring on the conservative side, he figured that he could generate roughly 25 pages of advertising a month in the first year of publication, 50 pages a month in the second, and 75 pages in the third. Within three years, *Essence* would be solidly in the black.

But Smith quickly discovered, as far as advertising was concerned, he was in a desert—and there was no oasis in sight.

We thought that our projections made sense. In reality, there was something that we didn't factor into the equation. It's what I characterized as the price of the paint job. I didn't properly estimate the resistance factor to companies advertising in a black publication. In the late 1960s and 1970s, corporate America felt guilty about the state of African America as a reaction to the protests and riots, but they didn't feel so guilty that they would take a product like Pond's cold cream and advertise it in a black magazine. It was really amazing. We couldn't get any of the cosmetics and health and beauty aids companies to advertise.

Smith knew he had to do something or the venture would fall apart. He was, after all, a master salesman. A closed door had never stopped him before.

If the cosmetics and fashion industries shunned black women, he would have to discover a new wellspring of opportunity. *Essence* was in the unique position of serving two audiences, women and blacks. He began to focus on companies that actively pursued black consumers—those in the automobile, tobacco, liquor, and travel industries. It would mean that he'd have to butt heads with John Johnson's *Ebony* and *Jet* and a slew of black newspapers. So be it. Determined, Smith stormed Madison Avenue.

He quickly secured cigarette ads, which had been forced off the tube and desperately needed new venues. But how was he going to win over the Big Three automobile manufacturers? They believed theirs was a man's world. African Americans were important to the new car industry, however, and Smith was an expert on the precious feminine slice of the $100 billion black consumer market. Smith challenged Detroit's perceptions head-on. While they might not consider the women's market to be important, he said, they simply *had* to embrace black female consumers. To capture African American auto buyers, they must realize that black women fully shared the decision-making role in the household, since most black families relied on two incomes. Ford, Chrysler, and General Motors would all miss out on a big opportunity, he said, if they didn't target a segment that held great influence on such purchases. He got his pages.

Smith's tactic broke new ground. Until *Essence* came along, it was unheard-of for companies to place ads for such big-ticket items in women's publications.

> *We used our unique quality to get different types of ads. When the auto industry started recognizing women's magazines around 1976, we were the only ones who could say that we can give you both—blacks and women. Through some rather inventive selling, we were able to get advertising in our book at a time when we couldn't even prove who our audience was. One of my greatest frustrations was that we did not have any market research on the magazine. For three years, we didn't have anything but imagination and creativity to sell with.*

Although *Essence* was still in survival mode, Smith's approach helped drive $2 million into the company coffers in 1972, making it the 63d largest black-owned company in the nation.

It wouldn't be the last time that Smith would have to be the rainmaker in dire circumstances.

Smith Rule #1: Make Sure You Have What Your Partners Lack

Smooth as silk, Clarence Smith is the consummate salesman. For 35 years, he has been able to inveigle advertising or investment capital from a prospect seated across the table. From his well-appointed office overlooking New York's bustling Times Square district, the articulate, dapper entrepreneur with dark, chiseled features plots new ways to market the brands of Essence Communications, Inc. (ECI). His efforts have helped transform a single niche publication into a $105 million media octopus with tentacles in publishing, television production, mail order, and music festivals.

Don't ever take his warm, gregarious nature for lack of

killer instinct. Nimble and dynamic, at 65 he's a heat-seeking missile targeting the next moneymaker, whether it's capturing new readers with a fresh magazine or hawking products in cyberspace. Over the years, he has developed canons on how to make a sale and run a business, all framed by his philosophy of "doing well by doing good."

In many respects, he is the polar opposite of his partner, CEO and publisher Edward Lewis. Usually Lewis's name precedes Smith's when paired. But that has never mattered to Smith. Their shared corporate vision has forged an unfaltering 30-year partnership, the longest such relationship among the B.E. 100s. In fact, it is perhaps because they are so different that they have worked together so well. The two have grown the company to its dazzling present-day height despite a history of vigorous outside competition and internal conflict.

Smith Rule #2: Plan Your Work and Work Your Plan— and Be Willing to Make Adjustments

Smith was reared in New York's blue-collar Williams-bridge section, a neighborhood that resembles the one in the movie *A Bronx Tale*. Though times were tough, young Clarence Smith, the third of four children, was "spiritually rich." His father, a janitor who delivered dry cleaning on the side, and his mother, a domestic, instilled in him a sense that "we could be anything we wanted, including president."

The idealistic words of encouragement, however, did not spare him from the harsh realities of job opportunities for ambitious black men in America.

While in his early 20s, he spent his days as a freight forwarder for a customs agency. But in 1963, a friend who sold him an insurance policy was impressed by his extroverted nature and sharp mind, and tried to lure him into sales.

The notion intrigued Smith. But breaking into the mainstream insurance industry proved challenging. The firm in which Smith sought employment was Prudential Life Insurance Company, which had only two African

Americans in its sales force of 55,000 representatives. Both had barely-brown complexions.

In those days, major insurance companies did not hire black insurance agents. The person who sold insurance to me was very fair-skinned. I grew up with him. When he told me about the opportunity, I had to check it out. I was very unhappy with my current situation. I was struggling to make a living and support my family. The work presented no challenges of any sort. He introduced me to a field manager who gave me a chance to take the insurance test. After I passed, he said, "I'll hire you, but you have to accept my challenge. You must be successful." I took his challenge.

Prudential gave him a stipend of $95 and eight weeks to sell a load of policies. The new recruit wasn't given a desk or phone. He could make sales calls only when a colleague left his desk. Smith wasn't about to settle for second-class status. His goal: to break into the exclusive Million Dollar Club, reserved for Pru's top performers.

His plan involved working seven-day weeks, cold calling from home, and selling policies to his network of acquaintances, friends, and family. Within a year, he sold more than $1 million in policies.

His reward: a desk and a phone.

Smith continued to rack up sales, proud of his achievements and secure in the belief that he could make a good living and a successful career for himself at Pru. Then, one day, he went on a sales call that forever tarnished his view of the industry.

In fall of 1964, in pursuit of large accounts that would earn fatter commissions, he went after Freedom National Bank, the black-owned Harlem institution cofounded by African American baseball legend Jackie Robinson.

He met with William Hudgins, the bank's president.

Before Smith could finish his presentation, the banker interrupted him. "I will not buy any insurance from your company."

Startled, Smith asked why.

"Because these insurance companies engage in redlining," he said, explaining the discriminatory process by financial institutions to refuse coverage or charge higher premiums to companies and individuals in minority and low-income communities. "These companies make a great deal of money from Negro customers, but they don't finance or do business with Negroes."

For an hour, Hudgins schooled Smith on how majority firms overcharged black customers and how black institutions, including Freedom National Bank, gained zero consideration when it came to getting business from them.

Smith was devastated. He had no interest in being a party to shortchanging black folks. He vowed to get out of the insurance racket, and, until then, to find a way to enrich his customers. While continuing to work for Prudential, he became a registered representative with the Investor Planning Corporation, a financial services firm. Instead of just selling policies, he put together financial packages for his black clients so they could build wealth by extracting the value from their whole-life policies and investing the money in mutual funds. It was a small way to appease his conscience.

In 1968, the country was gripped by wrenching events—and Smith's soul-searching grew deeper. Dr. Martin Luther King and Bobby Kennedy were assassinated. Frustrated African Americans rioted in urban centers. Corporate America sought to extinguish the flames. Times were definitely changing, and the 35-year-old insurance agent wanted a major change, too.

> *My son was one year old and I remember asking myself, "What is my son going to say to me 20 years from now? What would I tell him when he asks me, 'What were you doing during the struggle?'?" I didn't want to say that I was just selling insurance. It wasn't acceptable to me, so I knew that it wouldn't be acceptable to him. But I still didn't have a way to get out of it. If I was going to start a business, I needed capital. As I asked myself these questions, I found an opportunity to participate in something that could change the lives of black people.*

Smith Rule #3: Sell Anything, But Never Sell Out

These were the thoughts that propelled Smith to attend what would later be considered a historic meeting. In November 1968, two officials from Shearson & Hamill investment company—investment bankers Russell Goings, an African American, and Michael Victory, who is white—assembled a group of young black professionals to discuss the prospects of starting businesses. The incentive to attend the meeting was real: Shearson would offer financial and technical assistance for any viable venture.

As ideas were tossed around, Johnathan Blount, an ad salesman for New Jersey Yellow pages, raised his hand and suggested a concept for a black women's magazine. Actually, the idea was his mother's. She had once mentioned to him that "somebody ought to start a magazine for black women."

Smith thought so, too.

It was a revolutionary notion, he felt, that fit the mood of the times. The push for black empowerment had picked up steam and the women's movement was growing. Such a publication could capitalize on both trends. The traditional women's magazines, the dominant periodicals in the industry, weren't addressing the needs of newly liberated women and ignored black women completely.

After the meeting was over, the guys who were interested in the concept, which included myself, Johnathan, and Cecil Hollingsworth, talked about it further. Ed Lewis was not a part of that meeting. He would become involved at another Shearson gathering. After a month, we met at Cecil Hollingsworth's office and they offered me a job. They wanted me to come aboard as a salesman. I said, "Wait a minute, guys. I have a job. I'm making more money than any of you fellows. I want to be a partner and, if we get involved in this, we should all be equal partners." What was so unusual about it was that we didn't know each other. As I met with them, it became clear that

this could be a really great idea. None of us had a re-
alistic sense of what it would take to build a maga-
zine. We thought that after a year, we would give Time
Inc. some real competition. We thought that the world
was waiting for this idea and that if we could just get
the magazine out, advertisers would flock to it and
black women would buy it. We had no real idea how
difficult it would be. But I had made a commitment to
my wife, my family, and myself.

Clearly, Smith had the most to lose. He was earning big
bucks for that time—$30,000 a year. He had a growing
family and a house in the suburbs. In 1968 America,
most blacks would say that he had it made. But the need
to own a business and to make an impact outweighed any
fears or risks.

That entrepreneurial enthusiasm propelled us. Ed
Lewis came into the group slightly later and it is a good
thing that he did because he was a financial analyst
and a loan officer at Citibank. The reason why Ed
eventually ended up as chairman of the company is
that the people who were going to ultimately lend us
money wanted a feeling of security. Their feeling was
that they didn't know these black guys but at least one
of them worked for a bank and knows something
about the criteria for loans and the covenants in such
an arrangement. We all realized that none of us knew
anything about magazines, so we had to learn. We split
the tasks. Ed handled finance. Johnathan dealt with
editorial. Cecil investigated circulation. My job was to
develop a good list of advertising prospects and figure
out a reasonable market share for the magazine.

Smith talked to 15 ad directors from the nation's
largest publications, including *Time, Good Housekeeping,*
Cosmopolitan, and *New York* magazines. He prepared 10
key questions in advance and then grilled the ad directors
about the business. How did they establish advertising
rates? How did they make presentations to advertising

agencies? How quickly did they receive payment for advertising? And so on.

Smith spent hours in the public library thumbing through women's magazines, especially the so-called Seven Sisters—*Woman's Day, Family Circle, Good Housekeeping, McCall's, Ladies' Home Journal, Redbook,* and *Cosmopolitan*—and jotted down and categorized the ads that appeared in each issue. He researched their rates and set *Essence's* in the middle to avoid resistance from potential advertisers.

The partners developed a comprehensive business plan based on Smith's data and the financial, editorial, and circulation information compiled by the others. They further reviewed the plan with the publishing expert at J. K. Lasser, a New York accounting firm. After careful analysis, the four concluded that they needed $1.5 million to launch *Essence.*

The company was called The Hollingsworth Group, picked up from stationery that the print broker had left over from his graphics consulting firm. Initially, Blount served as president because he came up with the idea; Lewis, executive vice president and treasurer; Hollingsworth, vice president and circulation director; and Smith, vice president and advertising sales director.

Acquiring capital turned out to be a Sisyphean task. They made more than 100 presentations to bankers and venture capitalists. No one was ready to trust $1.5 million to four young black men with little publishing experience. To tide themselves over, they got cash the old-fashioned way: by borrowing money from friends. Personal loans totaling roughly $13,000 helped carry Lewis, Blount, Smith, and Hollingsworth through 1969, the year they left their full-time gigs.

Scouring the investment community, Lewis finally managed to persuade a consortium of banks and MESBICs (minority enterprise small business investment companies), including Citibank and Chase Manhattan, to seriously consider providing the company with some capital. The lenders, however, weren't willing to part with a penny until *Essence* had other substantial backers.

In late 1969, Lewis learned that Chicago-based *Playboy* magazine wanted to invest in new publishing properties. With other options exhausted, they had nothing to lose in pursuing publishing magnate Hugh Hefner. It seemed ironic that a magazine leading the charge for the independence of black women would hook up with the leader of the skin mags. To gain access to the mansion-bound Hefner, they convinced Jesse Jackson, the civil rights firebrand who lived in Chicago, to get Hefner's business manager, Robert Preuss, on the phone. To this day, Smith and Lewis will heed any request from Jackson because of that fateful call.

Weeks later, the *Essence* owners were meeting with *Playboy's* chief financial officer.

"How much money do you need?"

"We need $250,000," Lewis said, speaking for the group.

"How much equity are you willing to put up?"

"Six percent of the company."

"You want a quarter of a million dollars for six percent of the company," the CFO said, weighing the request for a few seconds. "I think we can do that. We'll get back to you."

A few days later, not having heard from Hefner, they met with the bankers. The partners told the consortium that *Playboy* was an investor, figuring the gambit would raise their confidence level and they'd leave the meeting with a check in their hands.

"So you got *Playboy* to invest in the magazine?" one of the bankers pressed.

"Yes, we did," said Lewis.

"I think that's great. I think we can go for it. Before I approve our commitment, I think I'm going to make a call to *Playboy* . . . right now."

As the banker left the room to make the call, Smith could feel his stomach churn. Was *Essence* going to sink before it left the dock?

The stone-faced banker came back and addressed his fellow colleagues. "It seems like we have a bunch of liars in this room. *Playboy* doesn't have a damn dime in this magazine!" he roared.

Smith could see the look of dread in his partners' faces. He felt the same sense of despair.

"We can kill this company right now or finance a bunch of guys with some really big balls," the banker continued.

The bankers decided to put their money on the gutsy entrepreneurs.

The partners received exactly $130,000. It wasn't $1.5 million, but it was enough to finance the first issue. In May 1970, *Essence* debuted. The press run was for 250,000 copies. Readers could buy the publication for 60 cents. On newsstands, the cover had a sledgehammer impact: a portrait-sized close-up of a hauntingly beautiful brown-skinned woman with a high, round Afro and a proud, vibrant smile.

Nobody had seen anything like it. Nobody bought it, either.

Although the cover was dynamic, sales were anemic. Eighty percent of the first issues were returned unsold. Neither readers nor advertisers were buying the following issues, either. Advertisers loved women, but they hadn't fallen for *Essence*. On the editorial side, the magazine had yet to find its voice. The partners fired three editors in chief during the first year.

Smith Rule #4: Raise Enough Money for a Cushion

Essence was strapped for cash. Forget having enough reserves for emergencies—they barely had enough to operate.

> *We asked for $1.5 million. We received $130,000. We were given just enough money to fail. The magazine was not going according to plan. Sales were poor. We couldn't generate advertising. We needed more capital. I was worried that we wouldn't make it. I was starting to get depressed. Ed's strength was working with Citibank and trying to gain financing from the MESBICs [minority enterprise small business investment companies]. I was trying to get advertising from categories outside of cosmetics, health and beauty,*

and fashion. It was a time when we figured out just about everything we had to do to survive. We used all of the tricks. We got the printer to finance us over five to six months in which he would charge us an interest rate on the value of the invoice. We quickly became known as the pariahs of the industry. In those days, if you wrote something for us or took a photo, you were lucky if you got paid. We made payment agreements with creditors and then reneged on them. They would call us or request payment; we would tell our assistants to tell them that we were out of town or not in the office. We would make partial payments on bills. We would trade suppliers and beg our bankers. We did, however, manage to make payroll. In order to survive, we had become hustlers. We quickly understood cash conservation. You don't go out of business because you don't make profits, which has a lot to do with accounting. You go out of business because you run out of cash.

Lewis was still negotiating with *Playboy* to obtain the proposed $250,000 investment. To gain capital, they sought funds from a variety of sources. Early on, they brought Gordon Parks, the famous photojournalist for *Life* magazine and the director of the movie *Shaft,* into the fold as the magazine's editorial director, enticing him with a few shares of company stock. Although Parks was placed on the masthead for name recognition, he didn't impress bankers.

It took 18 months for the company to get the $250,000 investment from *Playboy.* As the magazine began to build circulation and sales over the next two years, *Essence* was able to receive small amounts of funds from a variety of sources. Then, *Playboy* ponied up some financing. By 1974, a total of $2 million in capital came from MESBICs that included those associated with General Motors, Equitable Life, and General Foods.

They ultimately had a coterie of 10 investors in the company, but the *Essence* partners retained majority control. The financing, however, came with restrictions: The partners' salaries couldn't exceed $25,000 a year, they had to account for all money spent, and any major investment or purchase had to be approved by the consortium.

The covenants did not sit well with Blount and Hollingsworth, both of whom left the company in 1971 following a dispute over the rigid requirements. The two alleged that they ceded control of *their* publication to *Playboy*, although Lewis countered, "*Playboy* in no way tried to tell us what the editorial content of the magazine should be."

By 1976, Blount and Hollingsworth sued unsuccessfully to regain control of the company. Not surprisingly, by then *Essence* was a hit.

> *Ed and I agreed to the covenants. The principle behind it was that if you were willing to get rich in the end, then you should be willing to make sacrifices. It took us six years, instead of three, to break even. By 1976, we were $1 in the black. Just about that time, the original shareholders decided to sue us. They tried to place a restraining order on us and take over the company. It turned into a major fight. We were spending a lot of money on legal bills. Once again, we started having problems trying to pay off loans. It was an extremely difficult time for Ed and me. We didn't know whether we were going to win. We had to keep building the business and motivating the staff. By 1978, the court threw out Blount's and Hollingsworth's case.*

Smith Rule #5: Know Where Your Partnership Begins and Ends

Smith and Lewis are combat-close. In the 1960s, before the magazine was a glint in their eyes, Smith tried to pitch Lewis insurance. That meeting evolved into a close friendship. The ensuing years of trench warfare to keep *Essence* alive created an unshakable bond.

What made the partnership click was that the two men complemented each other so well. Lewis was the conservative banker who dealt with the financial community. Smith was the extroverted salesman who bagged the advertisers. Over three decades, those roles have held fast.

> *Most strong-willed entrepreneurs don't do well in partnerships. They tend to be inflexible. But you have to know your partners' strengths and weaknesses as well as your own. Ed's not very expressive, while I'm very expressive. I tend to look at the revenue side while Ed looks at containing costs. When he makes a point about costs, I recognize that strength. He has an appreciation for my strategies to drive forward new revenue streams. We're two different people, but we came to know and understand one another. We kept our egos in check because we were building a partnership, which is very much like a marriage. We also gave ourselves and colleagues the freedom to speak freely so that our egos would remain in check.*

With the internal struggle behind them and a new credibility in the marketplace, the two were poised to take the company to the next level. By the beginning of the 1980s, advertisers no longer had to buy razzle-dazzle. For several years, the magazine had been verified by the Audit Bureau of Circulation, which reported that circulation had grown to 600,000 and readership to 2.3 million. It was the third largest black magazine in the nation behind Johnson Publishing Company's *Ebony* and *Jet*. The annual advertising page count of 841 made it ninth among all women's publications in the country. On the 1981 B.E. 100 list, gross sales were $13.6 million, more than 600 percent above that of its first appearance on B.E.'s rankings.

The magazine's editorial voice grew strong and distinctive under the dynamic leadership of Susan L. Taylor, its editor in chief and grande dame. Hers would become the striking face of *Essence*, the earthy, yet polished, personality most closely associated with the publication.

Smith Rule #6: Teach What You Know

Finally, in the 1980s, Smith began to make significant inroads into the elusive cosmetics, health and beauty, and fashion categories and began assembling a crackerjack sales team. Since there were few African Americans in the general-market magazine industry—which is still the case today—he had to pluck talent from other industries and train them in ad sales.

I developed selling principles and taught people how to make a sale. I bought a nine-cassette set called "Nine Keys to Successful Selling" on the art and science of selling and made all my salespeople listen to it. During sales meetings, I would quiz them on points made in the cassettes.

The first thing that I had to get them to understand was that selling is not about conning someone out of something. It is about catering to a person's needs. Sales is a value exchange. The buyer always has to feel that the goods or services are worth more to him than the money he is taking out of his pocket. You have to convince the person why he is better off purchasing a product from you than anybody else. My program took away the concept of begging for ads.

Secondly, I communicated to my staff that a magazine like Essence *is a delivery system. It delivers compelling content, and through that content it delivers the reader to the advertiser. The advertising will resonate with the reader because of the environment in which it is placed. That's why they should advertise.*

Thirdly, premium value equals premium price. I told them never to apologize for the fact that your price stays higher than the other guy and that you never discount your price. Essence *is a premium value buy because the advertiser is buying into a premium market, the magazine of choice for black women. That is a value that is unduplicated. Those principles taught them confidence and gave them security. They were able to go out and sell the magazine with knowledge and passion.*

Most of all, I taught my staff that they had to have persistence. It may take you a long time to crack an account. Our toughest battle was to get Estée Lauder in our magazine. They thought that being associated with Essence *did not fit its upscale clientele and the higher price point of its products. We had to convince them that our readers would pay a premium for quality. It took us 22 years to break that account. As a result, other top cosmetic companies followed. We had to get the leader in order to get the others. They didn't want to be in a magazine with low price point products. You have to remember that in advertising, like everything else, companies want to be among their peer group.*

Smith Rule #7: Leverage Your Skills to Other Businesses

As the fortunes of the magazine grew, Smith was itching for diversification. First, he tried to convince Lewis and the board that ECI should expand into radio broadcasting. However, the directors quashed the idea because of concerns about costs.

In 1983, Smith tuned in to television. If he could develop a nationally syndicated show, hosted by Taylor, it would serve as an electronic version of the magazine and expose the brand to millions of viewers each week.

Producing the vehicle would be an enormous undertaking. *Essence*'s cash flow would pay for the show's production costs, but Smith had to sell enough ads to offset expenses and turn a profit. The catch: Sponsors would not pay for spots until they received affidavits indicating that their ads had been broadcast. By plane and train, Smith traversed the country, calling on program directors at stations in markets with sizable black populations. He had to achieve "a critical mass" of stations that represented 60 percent of the nation. Then, he targeted and pitched advertisers.

Smith was running a marathon. While he oversaw the television show, he supervised the production of *Essence*'s own series of television ads; managed the magazine's advertising staff; and opened sales offices in Chicago, Los Angeles, and Atlanta. But he received a big shiny medal at the finish line: In 1985, *Essence* exceeded its own expectations, marking its 15th anniversary with 951 pages of advertising and $15.3 million in revenues.

The Move to Greater Diversification

Over the next decade, Smith and Lewis endeavored to transform *Essence* from a single publication to a diversified brand synonymous with African American womanhood. The company launched a line of intimate apparel and a direct-mail catalog. The strategy: *Essence* would serve as the channel of sales for all of the new products. The goal: to develop products that would be custom-designed for the unique traits and tastes of black women (their skin tones, body types, facial structures, etc.).

We started developing products by paying attention to what was going on in the magazine. When we realized an increase in hosiery ads, we saw that as a product we could license under the "Essence" brand. The difference was that we would market hosiery that was anatomically designed for black women and had a range of color styles. When we marketed our eyewear product, the frames were an eighth of an inch longer to make sure that they fit black women more comfortably than frames that did not take their features into consideration. Not only did we seek to develop an array of products to meet the needs of black women, we customized them. We also sought to get to the market first. I always assume that we are not the only ones with the same good ideas. You always have to respect the competition and assume that they are smarter than you.

Smith Rule #8: Use Acquisitions and Strategic Partnerships to Grow Your Business

The success of their new ventures gave Smith and Lewis the confidence to expand into other territory. By 1985, ECI had taken an equity stake in Queens City Broadcasting, a $21 million B.E. 100 company that owned the top-rated ABC network affiliate, WKBW, in the Buffalo, New York, market.

By the 1990s, the Reagan and Bush Administrations had transformed the political climate into one in which the resulting shifts of attitudes on affirmative action and black Americans impacted their businesses. The 1970s and 1980s had been a struggle, but at least black publishers could get an audience with decision makers who listened to what they had to say. The constant frustration of not having *Essence* and its readers fully accepted prompted Smith and Lewis to consider launching publications that served the general market. As early as the mid-1980s, ECI began looking at general-market properties. By 1992, it acquired *Income Opportunities,* a general-market publication targeted at start-up businesses. Then, taking note of the burgeoning number of Hispanic consumers, it brought *Latina* to market in 1995.

But they never turned their backs on the *Essence* franchise. They expanded their licensed products through the Essence by Mail catalog, a strategic alliance with Butterick, a leading direct market firm. Another partnership, this one with Golden Books, one of the nation's leaders in children's books, resulted in the development of a series of books for young readers and their parents.

Smith Rule #9: Do Well by Doing Good

One of the biggest engines fueling the company's future growth is the Essence Music Festival, a three-day event that brings more than 170,000 African Americans to New Orleans each year.

The event, launched in 1995, has been Smith's baby. He worked with the city fathers on the venue. His sales team sold sponsorships. He brought together all of ECI's divisions to work on the programming and talent.

But, in 1996, it looked like it might turn out to be a one-year phenomenon. Smith and Lewis decided to pull the festival, which pumps millions into Louisiana's economy, out of the state unless the state legislature rescinded a proposed law that would ban affirmative action initiatives. Harking back to his disgust at the practices of insurance companies more than 30 years ago, Smith was not about to enrich a state that turned its back on his customers—or his people.

> *Ed and I made the decision that we could not in good conscience have black people celebrating in New Orleans one week and have their opportunities stripped from them the next. That is not what Essence is about.*

The state acquiesced to their demands, striking down the proposed legislation.

To remain successful into the next decade, ECI will continue to hold true to it roots—stay lean and nimble to take advantage of new opportunities, domestic and abroad. In fact, Smith and Lewis recently green-lighted development of Essence Entertainment, a new subsidiary that will find outlets to expand the brand in music, television, and interactive media. Also, the two have eyed prospective ventures in western Africa and South Africa.

To that end, ECI will pay for future projects by seeking bank financing, venture capital, and equity partners. While neither partner has plans to sell ECI, they haven't ruled out the option.

The key to the company's future will be developing the company's next crop of leaders. While neither partner has a succession plan, Lewis has no children and Smith's two sons aren't involved in the day-to-day affairs of the company. But that will not stop them from tapping the talent of the company's limited partners and employees—especially Taylor, the highly respected editor in chief. Part of the company's mission is to continue to bring black female executives to the forefront.

With the creation of new divisions and the infusion of talented executives, Smith is confident that ECI's brands will continue to flourish. That means Smith will have a larger stable of products to sell. A master salesman could not ask for anything more.

> *Essence is in good hands. We have the people. We have the brand. We have the vision. I'm even more excited than when I started.*

That infectious Smith enthusiasm remains his greatest asset.

RUSSELL SIMMONS: RUSH COMMUNICATIONS AND AFFILIATED COMPANIES

The Hip-Hopreneur

RUSSELL SIMMONS

Age: 41.

Birthplace: Queens, New York.

Marital Status: Married to Kimora Simmons.

Children: None (yet).

Education: Attended City College of New York, sociology major.

Entity: Rush Communications and affiliated companies.

Established: 1991.

Corporate Headquarters: New York, New York.

Products: Def Jam Records; Phat Fashions; *OneWorld* magazine; Rush Media; SLBG Entertainment; Def Pictures.

Number of Employees: 113.

Annual Sales: $40 million.

Mission: To market hip-hop music and culture globally.

First Career Move: Manager and concert promoter.

Role Models: His father, Daniel; Quincy Jones; David Geffen.

Simmons's Basics: *Be patient and learn everything you can about the business that you're entering. Hire people who are smarter than you. Find 'rabbis' to teach you what you need to know.*

On Money: *[When] I made my first $300,000, I was actually more excited about that milestone than when I made my first million years later. I was young and, up to that point, had made no more than $30,000 a year.*

On Race: *I don't allow myself to feel uncomfortable about being the only black in the room. That type of environment raises the bar for me. I don't want to be a big fish in a little pond.*

Regrets: Losing the white rap act, the Beastie Boys, in the dissolution of his first partnership to Rick Rubin.

RUSSELL SIMMONS:
RUSH COMMUNICATIONS AND
AFFILIATED COMPANIES
The Hip-Hopreneur

I want to keep rap and hip-hop culture real. . . . I believe that black culture is for the world.

Russell Simmons is a perpetual B-Boy. At 41, he still wears baseball caps and sneakers to business meetings. He doesn't give a damn if his profanity-laden speech isn't appropriate for the boardroom. He's *street*—and proud of it. Many of the nation's most powerful CEOs have come to accept the clothes, slang, and attitude. After more than 20 years in the music business, he's got bank. Loads of it.

With a net worth estimated at $100 million, Simmons has not only made millions with platinum artists and gold records, but he has done something few people in history can claim. He actually created an industry: hip-hop.

The bald, baggy-jeans-wearing CEO of Rush Communications has taken hip-hop's music and style, and crafted a diversified media conglomerate that includes a record company, four music publishing subsidiaries, a motion picture production company, a fashion house, a television division, and an advertising agency. Simmons stitched together these entities—mostly through joint

ventures—to create "dynamic and urban-based entertainment that captures the energy of the American youth
culture." So influential is his name in this market, it has
become its own brand; Simmons's name is a stamp of urban authenticity.

The company grossed $40 million in 1997, making it
the second largest black-owned entertainment company
in the United States. But Simmons calculates that the
sales of his products will push Rush past the $200 mil-
lion mark before the next millennium.

Simmons Rule #1: Play by Your Own Rules

For years, black entrepreneurs have been told that if they
want to be successful, they have to wear pinstripes and
earn M.B.A.'s. Russell Simmons built his empire on his
own terms. Often compared by the media to Berry Gordy,
of Motown fame, Simmons says he patterns his corporate
approach more after David Geffen, the openly gay music
mogul who also adopts a play-by-his-own-rules mentality, and who, in the process, has built a string of colossal
businesses. As for Rush, Simmons emulates megamodels
such as Time Warner or Disney.

In recent years, Simmons has summered in the see-
and-be-seen Hamptons, attending parties packed with
A-list moguls and celebrities. Why is he in such great
demand? Anybody who wants to know about urban culture seeks his viewpoint. Actor-director Warren Beatty
couldn't complete his movie *Bulworth*, about a politician
who embraces hip-hop culture, without it. Beatty actually camped out in front of Simmons's home to get the
411 on rap.

> *I talk to people like Donald Trump and Geffen every
> other day. I have developed relationships with them,
> gone to their homes and visited their businesses.
> These are people who deal with billions of dollars. I
> have gained that access and I use it. I don't allow my-
> self to feel uncomfortable about being the only black in
> the room. That type of environment raises the bar for*

me. I don't want to be a big fish in a little pond. My record company may gross $120 million or my clothing line may make $50 million, but that's not enough. That doesn't inspire me. I want more.

Simmons Rule #2: Pay Attention to Details

It's the spring of 1998, and Simmons is back home in New York after spending two years in Los Angeles producing movies like *The Nutty Professor.* Operating out of Manhattan's trendy SoHo district, Phat Farm, his five-year-old apparel division, is housed in a cavernous space that combines traditional Americana with sleek, steely gloss. "American Flava" is how Simmons describes the decor. Prominently displayed above its barn door entrance is the Phat Farm logo, an upside-down American flag with the face of an angry bull in its center.

Moving from one room to the next, he inspects baseball jackets, T-shirts, and sweatpants in rapid-fire succession. "This looks ill . . . too many buttons," he says, eyeing a utility jacket.

"Let's make sure that this golf shirt is crimson and cream and that the other is cobalt and orange."

As he drifts into another room, he takes a phone call on his omnipresent cell phone while examining a pair of cotton sweatpants that double as slacks. "I like those. They are the sh—"

The pants, the passionate opinions, the profanity—all are vintage Simmons. Thriving on the frenzied atmosphere, he makes time to talk to his designers about the new line. He looks down at his pink Phat Farm golf sweater.

I know what I want. I make clothes for myself. At the same time, I listen to the designers. They're very talented and smarter than I am.

He leaves Phat Farm and walks across the street to Def Jam Records, the crown jewel of his empire. He is immediately pulled into a room by a record producer full of energy and swagger who pops in the latest compact disc by a red-hot rapper called DMX. The music is loud enough to shake the walls. Simmons bobs his head back and forth to the beat and smiles as a sign of approval. He leaves the office, greets employees, asks for suggestions, and takes quick meetings in the corridors. Then, he's off.

The company's appropriately named Rush, derived from his childhood nickname. Simmons always was and always is in a hurry. Not much of a numbers-crunching administrator, he's a creative visionary who knows the hip-hop market inside out. He should. He invented it.

> *I want to keep rap and hip-hop culture real. But I believe that black culture is for the world. I don't want to [just] sell black people to black people. About 70 percent of our products are sold to nonblack consumers. We want to take this global.*

Methodically, he has catapulted his company ahead by consistently following three main strategies: finding mentors in new industries, developing a strong network of contacts and the best talent possible, and establishing partnerships to expand his business. But it would take him two decades to successfully use these elements to propel his company.

Simmons Rule #3: Find a 'Rabbi' to Teach You the Ropes

It all started with the beat.

As a teenager, Simmons rocked to the hard-edged, bass-heavy style of rhymes and rhythms that could be heard on the streets of the Bronx and Harlem in the late 1970s. He brought the grooves back to his neighborhood, the Hollis section of Queens, New York, a black working-class community with a smattering of professionals. His father, a professor at Pace University, was one of them.

In 1979, Simmons was a sociology major at City College of New York. To make extra cash, he orchestrated campus rap shows. Rush Promotions, his company, was a one-man operation: He found the acts, arranged the venues, and handled the marketing. In the beginning, he was so broke that he asked rappers to perform for a piece of the gate take. The rappers' popularity grew, as did Simmons's reputation. But few saw in their local success what Simmons saw: the opportunity of a lifetime.

> *I was promoting parties and concerts that featured Grandmaster Flash, Kurtis Blow, and D.J. Hollywood, many of the original artists before they became recording artists. A lot of people think that Rush happened overnight. But I had to have patience. I let the company grow organically and seized opportunities as they came. I spent several years in club and street promotion before I made one record. If you have a vision, you have to stick to it even though other people don't see it.*

In the 1980s, Simmons found his first mentor at one of his concerts: Roger Ford, a record producer who scouted for talent. Simmons peppered him with questions about the industry. Ford shared the basic principles of artist management. Among them, find a distinctive trait to make artists marketable, and when booking an act, hire an entertainment attorney to review the contracts.

> *He taught me that I should have a full understanding of any business before I pursue it. Every time I go into a new venture, I find a 'rabbi' who has the business acumen to help me understand the mechanics of that industry, the costs involved in developing a product, and what you need to do in order to make a profit.*

Out of 20 acts, Simmons's breakout artist was Kurtis Blow, a performer whose scatological raps produced a huge following on the college concert circuit. Ford suggested the promoter test the waters: release one of Blow's songs, "Christmas Rap," as a single. It proved to be fortuitous advice.

In 1984, Simmons was in the process of developing his

own music label when he got the brainstorm of teaming with Rick Rubin, a rich white college student from Long Island and a huge fan of rap music. Rubin had started his own record label, Def Jam (which, in street parlance, means "cool music") and operated it out of his dorm room at New York University. The two clicked. Russell had the acts and Rubin had a company that was already up and running. They became partners, investing $2500 apiece— Simmons's half came from his management income—to underwrite the first single: "Christmas Rap."

Simmons's mentor, Ford, helped them produce the record. Simmons engaged in grassroots marketing, selling records at parties, from his car, just about anywhere. Then, a breakthrough: Ford arranged for Simmons to meet disc jockeys at black radio stations to get airplay and expand the audience.

Selling more than 50,000 records, Blow's single was a hit. It became the first step in transforming Def Jam from a mom-and-pop label to an independent record company. By 1985, Def Jam was selling close to 500,000 records, and Simmons was about to have one of the biggest meetings of his life.

Executives at CBS Records noted the growing popularity of rap music and became interested in the upstart company, offering Simmons and Rubin a $600,000 deal. It worked like this: The young partners would produce records, while CBS handled distribution, marketing, and promotion. Def Jam would receive royalties on record sales. They went for it, launching 17-year-old LL Cool J and his first single, "I Need a Beat." It sold a million copies.

> *It was great. We thought that we were living large. I made my first $300,000. I was actually more excited about that milestone than when I made my first million years later. I was young and, up to that point, had made no more than $30,000 a year with the promotion business. We quickly learned the meaning of sound money management. We didn't track our cash flow properly, and moved into a big, impressive office.*

Within months, we were unable to pay rent and we were kicked out. From that point on, we kept our operation small and tight until we could afford larger quarters or additional staff.

As the two became more adept at handling their business, they developed a reputation as the dynamic duo of rap. Rubin produced the records while Simmons managed rap acts like Run-DMC, Whodini, Beastie Boys, and LL Cool J. On the prowl for talent from the club and party circuit to his old Hollis stomping grounds, he came to understand the symmetry of managing the talent that Def Jam recorded. He molded his performers, finding the right image and attire for each act. For instance, Run-DMC had a menace-to-society vibe, wearing black leather and heavy, braided gold chains, while the Beastie Boys, a white rap act, took on a more grungy persona. This all-encompassing Svengali approach earned him the Berry Gordy comparisons.

As white promoters began to compete for rising stars, Simmons held on to his acts because he could relate to them. He literally walked their walk. Everywhere Simmons went, including business meetings, he dressed like his performers, spoke the same raw language, and held the same aspiration: He wanted to be *huge.*

I decided that I was going to conduct business any way I wanted. The jeans and sneakers were my connection to my talent and customers. Young entrepreneurs come up to me to tell me that they admire my style and don't want to do business the conventional way. They don't want to do business in a suit and tie. I say that's fine but you have to be able to build relationships and communicate. If you can make the connection the way that I dress, you can do it. If not, you have to get what you want by playing by a different set of rules. As Def Jam became such a force in the music business, it didn't matter how I dressed.

The music and style of rap, he believed, could be commercial beyond the music industry. All he needed was a vehicle to test his theory. It came in the form of shoes.

Simmons Rule #4: Go After Your Least Likely Customer

One day in 1987, Simmons was in the studio, listening to Run-DMC cut their latest record. The group held a special place with Simmons because his brother, Joseph—better known as "Run"—was one of its lead rappers.

When Simmons heard the chorus of the song—"My Nikes"—he came up with a novel idea.

"Hold up," he said, signaling the three young rappers to stop. "You know, we should probably change the lyrics."

"What do you mean?" asked Run.

"If you change the lyrics from Nikes to Adidas, I bet I can get them to sponsor the tour. I don't think we would be able to get the same type of deal from Nike."

After the new lyrics were recorded, Simmons met with executives from Adidas. They didn't know what to make of Simmons, who was dressed in jeans, a T-shirt, and unlaced sneakers—the style worn by his young, hip audience—or his idea. Simmons was unfazed.

He told them about his hot rap group and how their new song was powerful ammo for Adidas in the ongoing sneaker wars. Nike and Reebok had athletes. Run-DMC, he explained, had more "street credibility" than any jock they could find.

The executives were not sold. They were skeptical about whether rap musicians could attract customers into a sports apparel outlet. Simmons invited them to the next Run-DMC concert. Reluctantly, the suits accepted.

Not surprisingly, the executives looked edgy sitting in the noisy, smoke-filled arena waiting for "their song." It was not exactly the prime environment for clamping a deal.

Then, Run-DMC yelled out, "Okay, everybody in the house, rock your Adidas." On cue, three thousand pairs of Adidas shot into the air. The executives agreed to sponsor the rest of the tour.

The Adidas deal only fueled Simmons's relentless pursuit of his crossover dreams. Despite all obvious evidence to the contrary, Simmons believed rap music could maintain its hard edge and still attract a broader (aka white, upscale, even global) audience. He tested it by teaming Run-DMC with the rock group Aerosmith, to record "Walk This Way." The scratching of rap met the squealing bass of rock and roll. The video produced for the single featured dueling artists in the beginning; by the end, Run-DMC and Aerosmith were performing arm in arm.

The message was loud and clear: Rap and rock could coexist, and be appreciated by both audiences. The result was just as positive: The first rap crossover was a solid platinum success. It forever changed the world of hip-hop.

Simmons Rule #5: Go for Mainstream Dollars

Run-DMC was not the only Def Jam act rocking the top of the charts. The Beastie Boys' *Licensed to Ill* sold 5 million copies and became the first rap album to reach No. 1 on *Billboard*'s pop chart. And LL Cool J's *Bigger and Deffer* album sold 2 million copies.

By the late 1980s, rap music accounted for roughly 5 percent, or nearly $400 million, of annual recorded music sales. Once considered too hard-core for universal consumption, it had clearly started to permeate the mainstream. Madison Avenue began using the gritty music to promote everything from fast food to appliances. It peppered Hollywood movie soundtracks. Rap videos, once scorned by music video channels, were among the most popular offerings of cable stations like Black Entertainment Television and MTV.

But despite growing popularity, rap specifically, and hip-hop culture as a whole, continued to be regarded by some as a fringe element at best, and utterly offensive and unacceptable at worst. Staying true to form, Simmons kept pushing the envelope, while also pushing for greater market share.

At the close of the decade, Def Jam's top act would be

the politically charged and socially controversial rap group Public Enemy. Ironically, the group, which featured militant Chuck D and Flavor Flav, a craggy-faced rapper who wore a huge clock around his neck, couldn't get airplay on black radio stations, let alone white ones. To promote the group, Simmons reverted to the methods of his college days, sending out crews of young people to "snipe"—plaster posters on billboards—and arranged for airplay in nightclubs and on college campuses. Word of mouth did the rest. Public Enemy's *Fear of a Black Planet*, released in 1989, sold 500,000 copies in just 10 days.

Motion pictures had become another means of promoting this music. In the mid-1980s, Simmons coproduced two films with hip-hop themes, *Krush Groove* and *Tougher than Leather.* Both were directed by Rubin and starred Run-DMC. Made on a shoestring budget, the films netted $5.1 million and $6.2 million, respectively. In other words, they flopped. But their soundtracks blew up.

For Def Jam to have a "phat" future, it needed a better arrangement from CBS Records, which had been acquired by Sony. The renegotiation sparked discord between Simmons and Rubin. Simmons wanted to use Sony's marketing muscle to propel Def Jam into other businesses, while Rubin wanted independence. They split the company's assets (Simmons took the Def Jam trademark) and its acts.

> *I was a manager and I wanted to establish new venues for my acts. I knew I couldn't do it without a company like Sony. One of my biggest mistakes in negotiating with Rick was giving him the most valuable act. The Beastie Boys was the top crossover act and I gave it him because he signed them. I still beat myself up over that one.*

Simmons Rule #6: Know What You Know; Find Partners Who Know What You Don't

Simmons fared better in his negotiations with Sony. In 1990, Simmons and Sony struck the first joint venture ever developed between a rap music company and an entertainment giant. In the old deal, Sony distributed Rush's records, pocketed the profits, and paid the label a royalty fee on each release. Now, Sony and Def Jam would split the earnings 50–50. To avoid massive overhead expenses, his agreement stipulated that the record company also pay Def Jam $3 million a year for operating expenses. The transaction gave birth to Rush Communications.

Before the ink was even dry, Simmons was itching to expand the franchise into uncharted territory. The next frontier: merging hip-hop with comedy.

> *Across the country, there were a lot of discos and rap music clubs that became comedy clubs for one night out of the week, and those nights were always sold out. That told me there was an interest in African American comedians, and I jumped in to service that market.*

Simmons had learned not to move on such ventures without a partner. He knew rap, not TV. This time, he linked up with two of Hollywood's hottest producers, Bernie Brillstein and Brad Grey, the team that developed *Ghostbusters* and *Wayne's World*. Then, he brought in Stan Lathan, a black veteran director, to co-produce the program and form Russell Simmons Television (RSTV). With top guns in place, *Russell Simmons' Def Comedy Jam,* a series of eight half-hour specials, debuted on HBO.

With its bawdy, X-rated humor, the show became the highest-rated cable program during its late-night slot. HBO was so excited by the ratings that it quickly sought to get the producers to develop 22 new shows. A phenomenal success, it launched the careers of such top comics as Martin Lawrence, Chris Tucker, and Bill Bellamy.

Like the movies Simmons produced in the 1980s, the comedy shows were done on a budget tighter than shoes that were two sizes too small. HBO paid the partners $2 million to produce 22 shows in 1992. All were made for under $500,000, a fraction of the cost to produce a sit-com. One reason was that Simmons acquired talent dirt cheap. As with his rap discoveries, he found rising stars who would give their eyeteeth to perform on a nationally televised showcase.

The show served two purposes: Simmons could make money and scout talent at the same time. To manage the careers of the Def Jam comics and pocket a 20 percent commission, he created SLBG (Simmons, Lathan, Brill-stein, and Grey) Entertainment. They mimicked the approach of Creative Artists Agency (CAA), the shop formerly headed by *über*-agent Michael Ovitz. Instead of searching for outside vehicles to showcase their talent, they would put together creative packages for their clients. That meant that Def Jam talent usually appeared in Rush productions.

Def Jam was still the company's cash cow, producing 10 gold, six platinum, and two multiplatinum records in 1991 and generating 60 percent, or $21 million, of annual revenues. And, despite controversy surrounding some of its artists, industry observers saw Def Jam as "the largest and most important rap label in the business."

Simmons Rule #7: Maintain Control of Your Market

The key to Simmons's success came from cornering the market on rap music and culture. In the beginning, major record companies thought rap was just a flash in the pan. Even some of Simmons's own managers contend that the company survived not because of its proficiency but because of its monopoly. Back then, nobody else was interested in the niche. But that was about to change.

Clarence Avant, one of the godfathers of black music and the force behind the creation of the B.E. 100s company Sussex Records in the 1970s, maintains: "Simmons [was] the main reason for the financial success of the whole hip-hop/rap music culture. If he hadn't gotten into it when he did, who can guess where it would be today. Not only is he one of the main reasons that so many people are making so much money from that culture, but he's also at the center of an empire that everyone wants a piece of. That gives him incredible clout in the power corridors of Manhattan and Hollywood."

That clout grew in spite of the fact that his management style remained unorthodox, to say the least. He rarely showed up at corporate headquarters, preferring to conduct business from his living room couch or from his bedroom. (Only one other CEO had successfully built a company from bed, and that was *Playboy's* Hugh Hefner.) Simmons's office was the telephone. There's at least one within arm's reach in every room of the $1.6 million triplex apartment he purchased from actress-singer Cher in 1990. He keeps at least one in each of his cars, from the Rolls-Royce to the Range Rover, and there's another one in his pocket at all times.

Simmons has long nurtured the ambition of becoming the most important figure in black entertainment. Of course, he has had to stand in line behind one of his idols, Quincy Jones, the multiplatinum record producer and entertainment conglomerator, and Bob Johnson, who runs BET. But, by the early 1990s, he was being bestowed royalty status with such titles as "hip-hop mogul" and "rap impresario." He was gaining a higher profile on the New York party circuit and through his own vehicles, regularly appearing on the closing moments of the popular *Def Comedy Jam*. He was also becoming visible through his philanthropic efforts in tandem with close friends, model Veronica Webb and short-term Motown CEO Andre Harrell. In any event, Simmons was having a blast.

At the same time, he was focused on doubling the value of his company. Like a handful of other black business owners, he began mulling over the benefits of an IPO. Rush had all the ingredients. A leader in hip-hop entertainment, the company had established successful partnerships to pursue new business opportunities. But Simmons knew there was no way the stodgy investment community was going to take him seriously as head of a public company. He didn't have the straitlaced corporate style and tight organization it looked for.

He needed professional management. Advised by a Wall Street financier, he hired Carmen Ashurst-Watson, a former filmmaker and fund-raiser. On her first day of work in September 1992, Ashurst-Watson met her new boss in the bedroom of his loft. Simmons was holding court: tending to the needs of recording artists and their parents and fielding business calls while being served breakfast and dealing with houseguests still recovering from a party the night before. Along with Yale lawyer David Harelston, Def Jam's president, she brought order to the chaos by tightening the company's structure, unifying the various units under one accounting system, and implementing strict financial controls.

Simmons didn't take Rush public, but these actions set the company up for its next stage of advancement.

Building a New Corporate Structure

By 1993, Rush no longer had a lock on its market. Major record companies, including Warner Records and BMG Music Group, had increased their market share through rap and hip-hop music. Clothing manufacturers like Tommy Hilfiger and Ralph Lauren began to capture droves of young African American purchasers and consumers true to inner-city fashion sense. Television studios established entire networks designed to capture urban viewers. Advertising agencies developed special units to create commercials and ads for this audience. In short, Simmons's crossover dreams became his urban nightmare—he spawned his own competition.

But he was determined to fight the giants toe-to-toe. BMG had Puff Daddy and Whitney Houston; he had Method Man and Foxy Brown. Hilfiger would have to take on Phat Farm. And, starting in 1996 Rush Media would compete against urban advertising boutiques. What helped Simmons shape this strategy was that Def Jam's success and influence placed him among a network that included Trump, Geffen, and other powerful businessmen and entertainment moguls. They formed an unofficial group of advisers whom he could use as a springboard for new ideas—and opportunities.

Simmons wanted to do things bigger than life.

As his deal with Sony was coming to a close, Polygram Entertainment came knocking on his door. Trounced by its rival, Warner Records, the company had acquired Motown for $350 million, but mismanagement and a string of hitless wonders made the company a poor investment. To establish a stronger presence in rap and hip-hop music, the company needed Rush.

In 1994, Simmons met with Polygram CEO Alain Levy and hammered out a deal in which the entertainment conglomerate would buy a 50 percent interest in Def Jam Records for $30 million—a stake that eventually rose to 60 percent. As in the Sony deal, Polygram would provide distribution support. The kicker: Polygram would also pave the way for Rush's expansion into film production. Simmons traded equity for the ability to compete with the big boys. Wedded to monolithic Polygram, he thought he could.

Inside his company, he maintained a mix of corporate professionals to oversee operations and young turks who kept their finger on the pulse of what was happening in the hip-hop community. He installed Lyor Cohen as president and COO of the record company—viewing him as a trusted liaison to deal with Polygram's executive suite—and an equity partner in Rush. A former roadie for Run-DMC, Cohen had been with Simmons for a decade, helping him sell 25 million albums as well as bring the next wave of chart-busting hip-hop acts like DMX, Montell Jordan, Redman, Method Man, and Foxy Brown to the forefront.

In 1996, Simmons and Anne Simmons, the company's senior vice president (no relation), formed Rush Media, LLC, a full-service advertising agency. Developing campaigns for the youth market, Rush Media leverages expertise from other divisions of the company. For example, the agency deploys the Rush Street Team, a service marketing and promotion company that identifies the lifestyle patterns and entertainment preferences of the 14-to-35-year-old urban tastemaker. The advertising firm quickly snared the coveted Coca-Cola account, being named its agency of record for the black consumer market. It was a major coup for Rush and a major blow to the more established black advertising firms. There was a new kid in town.

Rush Media's best-known work is a 30-second spot using the music of Marvin Gaye and Method Man during the 1996 Grammy Awards. That commercial, called "Father & Son," tested No. 1 among all youth that year. Since then, the agency has picked up ESPN and Revlon as clients.

> *We use our strength in the marketplace and interest in music to reach urban youth. Although the images are black, it is accessible to every consumer. The other agencies just don't have a feel for this market.*

As Simmons strengthened his base of employees, the relationship with Polygram began to sour. Since their alliance began, gross sales had grown a whopping 300 percent, but Simmons had become perturbed about Polygram's handling of Def Jam products and began making public statements about parting with his shares of the music division. Polygram's refusal to ante up $60 million for the remaining stake of Def Jam caused a war of words in the press between Simmons and Polygram CEO Levy.

Simmons even talked about cashing out his 40 percent stake, but his hands were tied. He's contractually bound until 2002. So, he's opted to make the best of it.

> *Say I sold Def Jam for $60 million. I would be able to live a bit more comfortably than I do now. Where's the excitement in that?*

He will seek to gain a stronger edge or a better deal with Seagram Company, which recently acquired Polygram's share of Def Jam as part of its $10 billion purchase of that company. Def Jam plans to work closely with the

Universal Music Group subsidiary, which has more of an affinity with Def Jam.

These days, Simmons's main focus is on Phat Fashions, which he created in 1992. The invasion of Tommy Hilfiger and Ralph Lauren into the urban market propelled him to defend his franchise. Phat Farm's clothing line, which is broken up into nine divisions, includes athletic wear and seasonal fashion lines. Sales have grown to $35 million, up from $13 million in 1998.

I see a lot of young entrepreneurs in the music business trying to rush out and start apparel lines. They figure that Tommy and Ralph did it, so can they. First, they have to learn the dynamics of the business. I made that mistake when I hired presidents to run Phat Farm who didn't have a marketing and licensing strategy. While they tried to figure it out, they spent hundreds of thousands of dollars. I was serious about being in this business; I had to learn it. I found two businessmen in the apparel business who became my mentors. In fact, they owned the company that licensed Phat Farm outerwear. They taught me how to inspect different fabrics and clothing design. I learned everything, right down to how buttons are sewn on products. They showed me the formula for marking up clothing. They told me the trade shows that I needed to attend. After I learned as much about the business as possible, we formed a partnership called American Design, which licenses all of Phat Farm's apparel. That way I have control over the quality and distribution of Phat Farm–licensed products.

The hip-hopreneur bristles at some of the treatment that he has received from some quarters of the fashion industry, which wants to segregate his line into ethnic clothing sections. For that reason, department stores don't get a stitch of his apparel. Instead, he has built the distribution slowly, selling in small specialty shops. Now, chain stores like Foot Locker are placing orders for Phat Farm apparel.

I don't classify my clothing as an ethnic line. I mean, my biggest seller is a pink golf sweater. It's not a dashiki or a grass skirt. I don't accept the concept of ethnic clothing. We have the same quality as Tommy Hilfiger or Ralph Lauren. I don't know what's ethnic about our clothing except that I'm ethnic and I own it. We don't want to have our products, whether it's film, fashion, or a magazine, pigeonholed. African American culture is mainstream. It's what the world has come to see as American. We want to fully participate in its marketing like every other company.

Byron E. Lewis: UniWorld Group, Inc.

Mr. Madison Avenue

BYRON E. LEWIS

Age: 67.

Birthplace: Newark, New Jersey.

Marital Status: Divorced.

Children: One child, Byron Lewis, Jr., president and senior producer of *America's Black Forum* (*ABF*), a UniWorld production.

Education: Long Island University, B.A., journalism; graduate studies in business and public relations, New York University.

Entity: UniWorld Group, Inc.

Established: 1969.

Corporate Headquarters: New York, New York.

Products and Services: UniWorld Advertising; UniWorld Hispanic; UniWorld Public Relations; UniWorld Direct Response; UniWorld Entertainment, which produces *ABF*; and Acapulco Black Film Festival.

Major Accounts: Colgate-Palmolive, Kraft Foods Inc., Ford Motor Company, and M&M/Mars–3 Musketeers.

Annual Billings: $162 million.

Number of Employees: 135.

Corporate Mission: To become the nation's largest multicultural advertising agency.

First Career Move: Ad sales for a now defunct black newspaper, the *Citizen Call*.

First Entrepreneurial Endeavor: Publishing the *Urbanite* magazine; it folded after three months.

Lewis's Basics: *You have to use all your strengths and know your weaknesses, and don't ever foreclose on any opportunity.*

On Networking: *Surround yourself with people who want to be somebody. It will help fuel your aspirations.*

5

Byron E. Lewis:
UniWorld Group, Inc.

Mr. Madison Avenue

Unlike black professionals today, . . . I was liberated enough to take chances [and] I was confident about one fact: I didn't know how to run an advertising agency but I understood the black consumer market.

UniWorld Group, Inc.'s downtown New York office, adorned with African art and vivid paintings, radiates with kinetic activity. Clusters of copywriters and designers—a mix of seasoned elders and young hotshots—work at a frenetic pace to roll out new campaigns for Ford, Burger King, and AT&T.

At the center of it all is Byron E. Lewis, the company's hard-driving CEO. Over 30 years, his efforts have yielded scores of awards and, more importantly, billings of $162 million, making UniWorld one of the nation's largest—and few surviving—black-owned ad agencies.

Lewis's presence doesn't immediately consume a room. Small in stature, he circulates, connecting with people one-on-one through endearing charm and laser-sharp focus. If interested in a person or a subject—his company and advertising are favorites—he lights up like a 100-watt bulb, spending hours in deep conversation. Says Alvin Gay, the senior creative director who left advertising giant

Ogilvy & Mather to work for him: "What turned me on about Byron is his passion."

At 67, Lewis is brimming with the same energy he expended 30 years ago in launching UniWorld. These days, he needs to draw upon those reserves as much as possible. When he started out, he converted Fortune 500 companies into clients by convincing them of the viability of the black consumer market. Now, general-market firms and young upstarts are invading his turf. But Lewis is confident of his edge over the competition.

We know the black community inside and out. Uni-World will continue to be the multicultural outlet to deliver ethnic consumers.

Lewis Finds His Way

From day one, it seemed as though Byron Lewis had been conferred underdog status.

Growing up at a time when racism snuffed out even modest dreams, Lewis wasn't immediately sized up for greatness, nor did he believe that the world had much to offer him. He never imagined he would be an entrepreneur, handling million-dollar accounts. And, frankly, he had no reason to envision such a future.

A child of the Great Depression, he was raised in the blue-collar Far Rockaway section of Queens, New York. Trying to make ends meet, his father, Eugene, worked seven days a week as a housepainter while his mother, Myrtle, a transplant from Galveston, Texas, cleaned homes.

Although his father was self-employed, young Lewis never considered business as an option. Rather, his aspirations sprung from his writing talent, which had earned him a spot on his high school newspaper. He thought he could make a career of it, majoring in journalism at Long Island University. But Lewis grew disillusioned when he found that major media didn't hire black reporters. He was drafted into the military.

I was in the Army for a few years and almost decided to stay in the military. In the 1950s, the Army had the most impact on African American men because it was integrated and black men were able to compete with white men on an even keel. It was really the first level of corporate training that blacks received because the service taught you to compete on a lot of different levels. You were able to manage men and money as well as provide leadership. When the affirmative action days came, army officers were among the first [black] people that I saw going into corporate America.

But journalism maintained its pull on Lewis so, in 1958, he once again pursued a job as a reporter at one of the mainstream newspapers. Still shut out, he went to the black press and landed a job at a Harlem-based newspaper, the *Citizen Call.* But there were no openings in the newsroom. He had to sell ads.

Lewis admired the *Call's* publisher, John Patterson, who had launched a mutual fund for African Americans and financed the newspaper through a stock offering within the community. Patterson was the first African American businessman with whom Lewis had close contact, and he was duly impressed. As often as possible, he would pick the publisher's brain. Lewis soon wanted the paper to succeed as much as Patterson did and clocked long hours in his attempt to break new accounts. But the resistance from white advertisers was too great. The *Citizen Call* shut its doors in 1960.

With his out-of-work colleagues, Lewis launched his first venture—a magazine called the *Urbanite.* It was geared to "the emerging Negro who had aspirations to be somebody"—in other words, people like him. Short on cash and advertising, the publication went belly-up in three short months.

Those years were a critical part of my development. At that time, all of the black businesses were in Harlem. I got a great education working around a lot of other talented black people, including Percy Sutton, a lawyer who went on to become Manhattan borough president and an entrepreneur in his own right;

Richard Clarke, who ran an employment firm and be-
came the largest black executive recruiter; J. Bruce
Llewellyn, the deal maker who at that time owned a
liquor store; and our lawyers, Charles Rangel and
David Dinkins, who went on to become a congress-
man and the mayor of New York, respectively. On any
day, you could see Adam Clayton Powell leading a
boycott of a store or Malcolm X giving a speech.
Harlem was a wonderful place to be around black
people trying to break through barriers. I was sur-
rounded by people who wanted be somebody. It fu-
eled my aspirations.

Although the *Urbanite* folded, it intensified Lewis's passion for the media. It spurred him to study business and
public relations at New York University at night while taking ad hoc jobs in sales and promotion during the day
and selling classified ads for the *New York Times* on weekends. The grind took its toll, but the hard knocks ultimately paid off.

It was all trial and error. I had a succession of jobs but
nothing that really stuck. I was very depressed be-
cause I was unable to make a decent living. In later
years, I realized that I was building a set of skills that
would become useful in my business.

In the early 1960s, he found jobs that suited his talent
and seasoning. He was hired by John Sengstacke, the legendary publisher of the *Chicago Defender*, to sell ads for
Amalgamated Publishers, a company that pursued national ad accounts for 153 black-owned newspapers
across the country. Then, Lewis became vice president of
advertising sales for *Tuesday*, a black-oriented literary
supplement in 14 metropolitan newspapers. In that position, he called on Madison Avenue agencies and urged
them to embrace the untapped black consumer market.
In most cases, he received the same frosty reception as in
his early days with the *Citizen Call* and the *Urbanite*. Account execs all but sneered at the thought of a black con-

sumer market. The very notion was simply too small and unsophisticated to matter.

Through sheer persistence, Lewis began to break the ad barrier. He personalized his pitches, telling prospects that he and his friends bought AT&T telephones, RCA television sets, Seagram's liquor, or Avon products—depending on which company representative was in the room. In some cases, he would produce letters from customers as testimonials. Then, he'd pull out hard data on *Tuesday*'s readers and figures on the black urban population and its discretionary income. In some cases, his approach actually worked.

In 1968, kismet intervened. Like much of America, the 36-year-old ad salesman reeled from the year's tragic events. In April, Martin Luther King, Jr., was slain in Memphis. In June came Robert Kennedy's assassination. Riots consumed urban hubs. Even the Democratic National Convention in Chicago was rocked by civil unrest.

These episodes impelled two professionals of Shearson & Hamill investment company—Russell Goings, an African American, and Michael Victory, a white—to hold a meeting as an attempt to stem the tide of black frustration through business ownership. In November, more than 50 black professionals were invited to that historic gathering (including Clarence Smith; see Chapter 3). Byron Lewis was among them.

As individuals stood up and discussed ideas for new business ventures, he thought about his future. He had years of experience working in the media. He knew there was a need for an advertising agency that would take black publications seriously. One that could educate majority companies about the black consumer market. One that could develop realistic and dignified black images.

Lewis decided he was the man to fill that void.

The Birth of UniWorld

He called his new venture UniWorld. One World.

His agency would bridge the gap between mainstream

America and the ethnic consumer. Even then, he thought about the eventual inclusion of Hispanic advertising. He had grown up with Latinos and they had faced the same exclusion from the media as their black counterparts. But that would come later.

First, Lewis needed capital. In the late 1960s, the public and private sector had created venture capital groups and minority enterprise small business investment companies (MESBICs) to finance the creation of black-owned businesses. Through his contacts, Lewis identified a potential backer. Connecticut-based venture capitalist Mason B. Starring and Fairfield Partners operated a private hedge fund to invest in and support new enterprises. Business plan in hand, Lewis enthusiastically spelled out his vision of UniWorld:

> *With the growth of the black consumer market, there needs to be a black agency that can help companies reach ethnic consumers. I want to be that agency.*

The financier was impressed by the dialogue. With a check for $250,000, Lewis was on his way.

Now in business, he just had to answer one critical question: What should he do next?

> *I started small, using shared quarters from another company. In the beginning, I had to take advantage of not knowing. I used whatever tactics it took and became a creative salesperson as a result of resistance by ad agencies to the black consumer market. When you go into business, you can't afford to carry an ethnic chip on your shoulder. Through the American Association of Advertising Agencies (AAAA), I set up meetings with the four leading agencies in New York to find out how to run a media department, how to manage accounts, and how much [to] charge for services. The most important thing that I discovered was that an advertising agency is a conduit of money and everybody gets paid before you do. Your reputation is based on your credit record so you have to engage in*

sound financial practices. In the whole process, the one thing that I didn't have to wrestle with was whether I made the wrong decision. It wasn't a risk because I didn't have too many options. Unlike black professionals today, who may feel [that] if they go into business they will risk careers, pensions, and liveli-hood, I was liberated enough to take chances. I was confident about one fact: I didn't know how to run an advertising agency but I understood the black con-sumer market. I had street experience.

But Lewis was smart enough to know that he needed much more.

It was imperative that he learn every aspect of the business. Advertising receipts are measured by billings, with gross revenues averaging between 10 percent to 15 percent of the total. Depending on the number and size of the accounts, one client reneging on payments or cancel-ing a contract can put a shop out of business—fast.

To his credit, Lewis wasn't shy about asking for help, or taking it. Among his first employees was the late Ann Mentor Killian, then one of the few black creative directors in advertising. As a college student, Killian met Lewis dur-ing his brief *Urbanite* stint. She liked the fact that he was a spark plug, a continuous source of bright ideas. She wrote him a letter, stating that if he ever started another business to count her in. Lewis took her at her word.

Black entrepreneurs coming into the business today should follow [a] key principle that I learned when I first started UniWorld. It still applies today. As they grow their company, they should find employees—on the business side and creative side—who are smarter than they are. I was able to find a creative director who knew about account management and the devel-opment of creative content. I found a business man-ager who watched over every penny in the company. In many cases, they came aboard not so much for money, but to learn and make a contribution. You need to carefully screen your employees at every stage. When you hire them, make sure that they have a commitment to your firm—and that you have the same commitment. UniWorld required my complete focus. If you are going to be in advertising and build a business, it is a 24-hour [day], seven-day [week] proposition. If [you are not up for it], you should look for something else to do.

Building up his base of clients was toilsome. Most of his prospects made clear their belief that selling to blacks was like pouring money down an open drain. Liquor companies, on the other hand, immediately jumped on the bandwagon, and Lewis chased these accounts. Smirnoff's, one of the companies that placed ads in *Tuesday*, was his first account.

He knew, however, that UniWorld would be buzzard bait if he relied solely on pitching consumer products companies. Those accounts needed to be cultivated over time—time that he didn't have.

He zeroed in on politics and entertainment, assignments that could keep money flowing into his agency. In 1971, his first campaign was handling the media strategy for Kenneth Gibson, who ran for mayor of Newark, New Jersey. Lewis's billboards, radio spots, and grassroots approach helped Gibson become that city's first black mayor. They also helped pay UniWorld's bills.

The next project allowed him to flex his creative muscles. Through a brief stint as a publisher for *R&B World*, a music magazine, Lewis had become friends with Al Bell, the visionary founder of Stax Records, a Memphis-based entertainment company with such artists as Joe Tex and the Staple Singers. In 1970, Bell conducted research on black patronage of the movie industry and found that they represented 20 percent of the audience supporting action films. Looking for new ways to promote his artists, Bell met with MGM about creating a black action-adventure flick so that he could produce the soundtrack. The movie became *Shaft*, Hollywood's very successful black detective film that kick-started the so-called blaxploitation era of motion pictures. Stax artist Isaac Hayes wrote the movie's score and Bell suggested to MGM that an African American agency handle the promotional campaign. UniWorld was Bell's first choice.

Lewis conjured up the bold image of the detective smashing through a window with a gun in his hand over the slogan, "Shaft's His Name. Shaft's His Game." The radio spots used the same tag line with Hayes's popular theme song blaring in the background. After the film raked in $15 million at the box office—a smashing success for the time—UniWorld was tapped to handle similar work for the film's sequels. UniWorld was now a success, grossing more than $150,000 in the early 1970s.

At this stage, most of Lewis's accounts were relationship-driven; they were carryover clients from companies that worked with him before he started UniWorld. In these early days, his firm survived largely because of the emergence of such black publications as *Black Enterprise* and *Essence,* both started in 1970; the dawning of the syndicated television show *Soul Train*; and the growth of black radio stations in urban markets nationwide. These venues provided him with outlets for his clients to make media buys, in which UniWorld would pocket a 15 percent commission.

UniWorld barely stayed afloat, but most black ad agencies sank. During the early 1970s, the U.S. Census showed that there were less than 25 black-owned ad agencies out of 7188 such firms in the nation. The mortality rate even for those few was staggering: Most survived less than two years. The situation became so dire in 1972 that Vernon Jordan, then executive director of the Urban League, addressed the American Association of Advertising Agencies: "Advertising agency billings reached a record $13.6 billion. A mere $100 million of that, less than one percent, went to black media. Black consumers generated billions of dollars for your industry, but the media that serve them—black newspapers, magazines, and radio stations that constitute the avenue of communications among black people—got less than one percent of total industry billings." Four years later, when ad agency billings ballooned to $26 billion, the black share of media dollars was still less than one percent.

Lewis was determined that UniWorld not become another business statistic, but his struggle to keep it going was a daily one. In early 1974, he obtained an additional $100,000 from a guaranteed Small Business Administration loan supplemented by a loan from North Street Capital, General Foods' MESBIC. It turned out to be stopgap funding.

Within months, he had fallen behind in his loan payments and struggled to pay overhead expenses. He desperately needed to secure more lucrative accounts. At a board meeting in late 1974, Lewis was forced to confront UniWorld's dire economic straits. After reviewing his financials, his directors told the 42-year-old entrepreneur that if he didn't make rain soon, he should shut down operations. Lewis felt as if he had been gutted.

After the session, Patterson, his old boss and mentor, took him aside.

"Byron, I know it looks bad," he said. "Don't think about what it takes to be a traditional advertising firm. You know black people. Think about the best way to reach them. Once you do that, the ideas will flow."

Still shell-shocked, Lewis took Patterson's advice to heart. It was the Christmas season, and, as he walked into the cold night air, it seemed a bit chillier than usual. If he didn't come up with a solution, it would be a frigid New Year.

Lewis found the answer in his own family. As they engaged in holiday cheer, he remembered past gatherings. His mother and grandmother would huddle around the radio, engrossed in the serial *Stella Dallas*. At the conclusion of each program, they spent hours talking about the mishaps of each character.

Could a similar format be designed for black folks? If it worked, revenues would come from the program's sponsor. Or, so the idea went.

I saw the need to create programming as a new way of reaching black consumers. During the 1970s, one of the prime entertainment vehicles was black radio, which was in its infancy. Percy Sutton's Inner City Broadcasting had developed New York's WBLS-FM and created the urban contemporary format that was being imitated by radio stations across the nation. I realized the opportunity and created a black radio series called Sounds of the City. *It was a soap opera about the transition of a Southern black family into the Northern environment and all the problems they had with jobs, drugs, and crime. I grew up hearing soap operas and it used to fascinate me how my family would actually live vicariously through the lives of these white fictional characters. I had not been successful in getting enough advertising in a traditional way to keep the company going. It was really a very desperate idea, but I had nothing to lose. What I discovered was that you have to use all your strengths and know your weaknesses, and don't ever foreclose on any opportunity.*

Lewis rolled up his sleeves, and got cracking. He hired writers and actors from local black repertory theaters, including then-struggling thespians like Robert Guillaume, who would later star on the television show *Benson,* and Lawrence-Hilton Jacobs of *Cooley High* and *Welcome Back, Kotter* fame.

Most of all, he needed to find a sponsor. Any company would do. But Lewis was intrigued by the possibilities of working with a food company with family-friendly products—unlike liquor and tobacco—and an array of different brands. It would give him the opportunity to try to snare several accounts from one company instead of trying to chase a number of accounts from a slew of entities. From his short list, he chose Quaker Oats, mainly because it sold products that were staples in every black household: oatmeal, cornmeal, pancake mix, and syrup.

He told Quaker Oats executives about his concept, recounting the impact that the soaps had on his family. Lewis suggested that the company could significantly bolster the penetration of its brands among African Americans through this unique vehicle on black radio. Intrigued, they decided to take a chance on Lewis's inspiration.

The series of 15-minute episodes ran five days a week, on 27 black-owned radio stations, from New York to Jacksonville, Florida. In the 39 weeks that it aired, *Sounds of the City* saved UniWorld, pumping in a much-needed $5 million in billings and becoming the agency's largest account at the time. Just as important, it bought Lewis time to attract new business and another $10 million in billings through the addition of such major accounts as the Environmental Protection Agency, General Motors, and R. J. Reynolds Tobacco Company to its client roster. *Sounds of the City* is long gone. But to this day, Quaker Oats is a UniWorld customer: The agency currently handles the $4 million Gatorade account.

> Sounds of the City *was innovative marketing. It was the first of its kind. We had to be innovative because none of the food companies would engage in traditional advertising with us. It laid the foundation for the company, a diversified business that could do several things. With Quaker Oats, we were able to handle promotions every day. We produced the program and then we began to develop the radio spots to promote the company's products. We ran commercials for all of the shows. We had every arm of the agency working on the show. Viewers listened to the program and Quaker Oats realized an increase in sales among black consumers. I came up with the idea of developing a broad-based communications company that can use a variety of techniques to reach the African American consumer. Above all else, it had to be mainstream competent— and competitive.*

The success of the program provided Lewis with cash flow, but, more importantly, it had bolstered his confidence. It was epiphanic: Lewis's vision shifted to remaking UniWorld into a multifaceted marketing machine that could develop print and television advertising, plan events, and create its own vehicles. For Lewis, diversification would not be an ingredient but the very recipe for his agency's growth.

Sounds of the City sparked other ideas for radio programs. It made sense for the agency to go this route: It reaped sponsorship dollars, commissions for placing ads, and fees for producing them. One show bore multiple revenue streams. Lewis sought partnerships as a way to defray costs and eliminate competition. For example, the marketing maven structured a joint venture with National Black Network, another B.E. 100 company at the time, for the first on-site black radio and press coverage of the 1976 Democratic and Republican presidential conventions. Such arrangements netted UniWorld millions in billings. The side benefit: The venture begat valuable, long-term relationships.

> *We were able to get AT&T as a sponsor because we convinced them that it was a way for them to reach the most influential and affluent African Americans. It was an exciting time for us. Georgia state senator Julian Bond was the host and we covered everything from the convention floor to the smoke-filled meeting rooms. Four years later, we coordinated all of the press activities for the first black political convention in Gary, Indiana, in which I was able to start the development of a strong relationship with Reverend Jesse Jackson. UniWorld really grew with the evolution of blacks in political power because we became a participant in that structure. I was tied into them. That led to us handling Jackson's first presidential campaign in 1984. These campaigns put us in good stead because we now have good personal working relationships with all of the African American leadership.*

Lewis had used revolutionary marketing vehicles to propel his agency, but he still hadn't broken into the lucrative arena of television commercials. Then, in 1975, Avon called. Impressed with Lewis's chutzpah, James

Preston, the company's chairman, believed UniWorld could enhance the company's image on the tube. Lewis's previous comment that "Avon representatives were one of the first constant black professional presences in many African American communities" stuck with him. It was just the type of message that he wanted to convey to black consumers.

> *Avon really took a leap of faith with us. I believe that the assignment, in part, was a function of their affirmative action initiative. We never worked on a television commercial before. We found the talent that could shoot the commercial and scrambled to make it happen. It gave us the experience to take the next critical step with our company. Television production was an important part of my strategic vision.*

The project fed Lewis's desire to develop television programs. In 1977, he formed UniWorld Entertainment, a production company that created such television shows as "This Far by Faith," a special on the impact of the black church for Reverend Benjamin Hooks, the executive director of the NAACP at the time; "Sweet Auburn" with the Martin Luther King Center; and annual telecasts of the Congressional Black Caucus weekends.

By 1984, such productions had prepared Lewis to produce an ongoing public affairs program. An offshoot of the 1976 radio program giving convention coverage, *America's Black Forum* (*ABF*) was a nationally syndicated program that focused on news and politics. Once again, he tapped Julian Bond as its host. To fund the program, Lewis received $35,000 from General Foods' North Street Capital MESBIC.

The challenge was getting stations to pick up the program. Lewis crisscrossed the country pitching program directors in major markets. It took years for him to gain commitments, winning one market at a time. Today, *ABF* airs in 70 markets covering 85 percent of U.S. households. As usual, clients, like Burger King and Ford, sponsor the program through ads that the firm developed.

As we developed more creative solutions to the challenges of the industry, my excitement about UniWorld and the possibilities just kept growing. I didn't see UniWorld as a personal sacrifice because I was doing significant things and meeting fascinating people. I wasn't living an ordinary life in an ordinary job. I remembered when opportunities were barren and I didn't know what I was going to do with my life. I found that advertising was a business in many different businesses. It was financial. It was strategic. It was marketing. It was creative. It was entrepreneurial. UniWorld gave me the opportunity to reinvent myself. It permitted me the opportunity not only to meet movers and shakers, but to know them personally.

And, to become one of them.

The Challenges of a New Era

UniWorld didn't expand because of its innovative approach alone. In the late 1970s, when an economic downturn threatened profits, more major corporations began to realize that future revenue growth would come from untapped market segments. The agency was poised to take advantage of these new dynamics. In fact, much of its creative and managerial employee pool came from talented but frustrated black professionals who bounced off the glass ceiling and through the exit doors of white advertising firms.

UniWorld, like the growing number of black ad agencies that cropped up in the 1980s, capitalized on its contacts, skills, and special understanding of black consumers. A new appreciation of market segmentation by advertisers produced bigger budgets for black consumer advertising. In 1985, the top six B.E. advertising agencies reported collective billings of $155 million, a figure that would have represented the total pie just 10 years earlier. A top player, UniWorld's take was roughly $40 million in billings. For the next 10 years, the company would repeatedly flip in and out of position as the nation's No. 1

advertising agency. Its main competition: Chicago-based Burrell Communications Group, led by another black dynamo, Thomas J. Burrell.

After years of preaching to white companies about black consumers, Lewis was finally validated in what could be described as the quintessential Kodak moment. In 1984, he captured a $4 million account with Eastman Kodak Company after the film and camera maker realized that the best way to protect its overall position as an industry leader would be through deeper penetration of black and Hispanic markets. It was a case of a mature company in a mature industry becoming more sophisticated about the realities of market share growth.

Around this time, Jesse Jackson and Operation PUSH, his economic empowerment organization, sought to develop greater opportunities for African American entrepreneurs through the creation of trade agreements. These accords would provide franchising and vending opportunities for minorities and increase marketing efforts with five major corporations, to the tune of more than $1.5 billion. One such company, Burger King, signed a $500 million agreement to increase business opportunities for blacks.

The ubiquitous Lewis pounced on the account, making a pitch to the fast-food operator to take over all of its black-oriented marketing assignments. He first gained the support of Burger King's Minority Franchise Association, a consortium of the company's black franchisees. The organization, in turn, pushed the company's management to hire the agency. The account became UniWorld's largest to date: $30 million in billings.

Coups come in many forms. The following year the chairman of Coors Brewing Company made a statement in front of members of the NAACP that blacks "should be happy that they were brought [to America] in chains." Hoping that money would talk louder than words, Coors agreed to spend $500 million with black businesses. The initiative paved the way for Lewis to land $5 million in billings from Coors. (In 1996, he would benefit from yet another corporate faux pas when Texaco increased its marketing to the black community after some company executives were found to have established a blatant pattern of making derogatory remarks to African American employees. UniWorld's take: $10 million in billings.)

A New Strategy for a New World

By the late 1980s, in a sense, black agencies had started becoming the victims of their own success. Although they were getting more work from existing clients, new accounts became resistant to hiring black agencies in response to the diminution of affirmative action policies. Large Madison Avenue firms, finally taking note of the fast-growing minority consumer market, began vying for black advertising dollars—successfully.

There's no doubt that without affirmative action, we wouldn't have gotten a foothold in the industry. Because of affirmative action, there were actually black people gaining experience in the advertising industry. In the early 1980s, I realized [there were] several developments that would ultimately change how UniWorld would operate. First, the Republicans saw that there shouldn't be the range of entitlements, as they called it. The hiring of black professionals tapered off in white companies and the glass ceiling dropped lower. Fortunately, we were able to benefit from a resource pool of trained black talent. Secondly, it became clear to me that there was the creation of a no-holds-barred environment. The mainstream agencies started competing for the budgets that black advertising agencies had developed without anyone safeguarding our territory. So it was clear in the 1980s and 1990s that the competitive threat to UniWorld would come not only from other established black agencies but also from mainstream firms.

While other black firms were looking at segments within the black community, Lewis began focusing on "micro-segments" in multicultural communities. Way ahead of the pack, he began directing clients to the burgeoning Hispanic market in the early 1980s. The result was the creation of UniWorld Hispanic, which produced spots to promote Mead Johnson's Nutrament drink and the Spanish edition of the *Daily News*—accounts collectively worth $4 million in billings. UniWorld Direct Response, a recently formed division, targets and markets products to slivers of black consumers, including those from the Caribbean and black professionals. As part of Lewis's synergistic approach, he has persuaded clients to become exclusive sponsors of the UniverSoul Big Top Circus, which reaches 1.5 million black families in 60 cities. In addition to helping black independent filmmakers get their movies screened, the annual Acapulco Black Film Festival was developed as another marketing vehicle for such clients as HBO and Eastman Kodak.

UniWorld's success rate has placed it in the enviable position of going toe-to-toe against major mainstream agencies—a rare occurrence for black ad agencies. The best evidence of this occurred in 1993 when Burger King fired its tenth agency within as many years and then called Lewis. For years, Burger King had been unable to develop a consistent marketing message and gain market share from its archrival, McDonald's. The company's top marketing officials offered Lewis a shot at competing for the national interim campaign while it searched for a full-time agency. Although part of the deal precluded UniWorld from consideration as the agency of record, Lewis hopped on the challenge.

The contest pit UniWorld against ad industry giant Saatchi & Saatchi. Lewis became personally involved and pulled in his best people. They went through scores of storyboards and slogans. Within weeks, UniWorld lanced its competitor with a spot for the Whopper. The tag line: "We May Not Be Number 1. We Just Taste Like It."

At a feverish pace, UniWorld developed over 50 commercials that ran from November 1993 to January 1994.

The spots enabled Burger King to maintain its first sustained sales increase over a six-month period and took a chomp out of the market share of the Big Mac. It was the first time that a black agency had pulled off such a marketing coup.

The success with Burger King led to another general-market account. In 1995, M&M/Mars, the huge candy manufacturer, awarded UniWorld the $11 million 3 Musketeers candy bar account. Even though it was a general-market campaign, UniWorld brought its urban sensibilities to marketing the product. The campaign features comic actress Fran Drescher, star of *The Nanny,* three swordsmen, and the slogan "Big on chocolate, not on fat." Since the candy bar was a favorite among ethnic consumers, UniWorld's creative team hired a black actor to play one of the foil-carrying characters. The campaign was a winner.

Fighting for the Future

While success breeds success, it also entices new and ever-intensifying competition. As general markets become saturated while ethnic markets continue to grow, both established firms and upstart agencies are aggressively pursuing urban and youth markets. In 1996, advertising giant DDB Worldwide teamed with black filmmaker Spike Lee to create Spike/DDB, an agency that develops campaigns targeted at that consumer. Russell Simmons's Rush Media, launched in the same year, is Coca-Cola Company's agency of record for the black consumer. And, the stodgy, old-line Chicago-based firm Leo Burnett Inc. recently spun off Vigilante, a funky, hip boutique agency aimed at a funky, hip consumer group.

It is still unclear whether UniWorld will ultimately win the battle for accounts, partly because it is unclear who will run the company once Lewis retires. He has a battery of senior executives who oversee various divisions, but he has not selected a successor or put a scheme in place for the inevitable transition of corporate leadership. His son,

Byron, Jr., serves as producer of *America's Black Forum*, but has no aspirations for heading the entire operation.

To grow his company, Lewis will continue to pursue his strategic vision.

> *My hedge against decline is that UniWorld doesn't de-pend on any one market segment. We can put our clients in the urban market, whether it is segments of the African American or Hispanic communities, or we can handle general-market accounts. We know we have an edge because mainstream popular youth cul-ture is primarily influenced by ethnic culture. It's ironic that we, the pioneers, must compete with mainstream agencies for our survival. But we're survivors and we're up for a good fight.*

MEL FARR, SR.: MEL FARR AUTOMOTIVE GROUP, INC.

The Superstar

MEL FARR, SR.

Age: 55.

Birthplace: Beaumont, Texas.

Marital Status: Married.

Children: Two sons, Mel, Jr., and Michael; and one daughter, Monet.

Education: Attended the University of California, Los Angeles; B.S., political science, University of Detroit.

Entity: Mel Farr Automotive Group.

Established: 1975.

Headquarters: Oak Park, Michigan.

Products and Services: New and used domestic and foreign automobiles.

Annual Sales: $573.1 million.

Number of Employees: 817.

First Job: Washing cars at his father's auto dealership.

Mentors: His father, Miller, Sr.; John Mallon, head of Ford's dealer development program in the 1960s.

Farr's Basics: *Stay liquid, make payroll, and put your money back in the business. Learn the difference between personal pride and pride in performance.*

On Salesmanship: *The customer is always right. Listen to [your customers].*

On the Winner's Mentality: *Winners visualize future success, cause change, focus on customers, continually improve, and hang with other winners.*

On the Art of the Comeback: *I decided that I was going to do anything to bring customers on [my] lot. A black guy in a cape was sure to get attention on television.*

6

MEL FARR, SR.: MEL FARR AUTOMOTIVE GROUP, INC.

The Superstar

Often pleased but never satisfied.

Mel Farr takes on every challenge with the same focus, speed, and dynamism that he had playing on the gridiron for the Detroit Lions. During his glory days, the prizes were most valuable player (MVP) awards, rushing records, and Super Bowl championship rings. That was then.

For nearly a quarter century now, Farr has been more of a fixture in Detroit's boardrooms than on its football fields. He has built a dynamo of a car sales business, with successful dealerships stretching from Michigan to New Jersey to Texas and back. What continually motivates him is a seemingly unquenchable desire for more.

More franchises.

More sales.

More money.

Driven by ego, he rewrote the playbook in the industry, and, in the process, drove Mel Farr Automotive Group, a $573 million enterprise that refuses to stop growing, to become the nation's largest black-owned auto dealership. His enterprise sprawls, requiring him to take his private plane, a Beechcraft King Air eight-passenger turboprop christened *Superstar II*, to survey his numerous holdings. The centerpiece: his 13-acre, 500-vehicle used-car emporium in Ferndale, a few miles outside of Detroit. The superstore fulfills Farr's vision of providing used cars to "the financially challenged," working-class urban dwellers low on cash and short on credit, but desperately in need of transportation. While most dealers chase affluent suburban customers, he pursues this sub-prime market—handling the financing of car purchases and making a hefty profit by charging steep interest rates to credit risks.

That's why this overcast day in early April 1998 holds so much importance. Like clockwork, Farr takes his daily two-mile run. It gets the juices flowing, clears his mind, and keeps his 54-year-old body rock solid.

As he jogs, he reflects on the news buzzing throughout Detroit. From the factory floor of Ford Motor Company to showrooms of local dealers, everyone is wondering about the meaning behind the resignation of Edsel B. Ford II, president of Ford Motor Credit, the financing arm of one of the nation's great automotive empires. This is, after all, the Motor City, a company town where a sudden management shift can affect thousands of people, whether they build vehicles on assembly lines, approve auto loans, or peddle cars.

Farr is no exception. In fact, he has a proposal hanging in the balance that would propel his exalted ambitions.

A few hours later, now nattily dressed, he struts into his five-acre Oak Park dealership, corporate headquarters for his automotive monarchy. He greets employees and customers. They feel the spark as the charismatic entrepreneur flashes his trademark 10-carat grin. It's the smile that has closed a thousand sales.

The office hums. Immediately swamped by phone calls and meetings, he conducts business in an easy, relaxed fashion. When he talks to staff members and makes a point, he speaks in a near whisper, forcing them to lean forward to *listen* to what he has to say.

As the morning wears on, he still awaits word from Ford Motor Credit. Then, at 11:15 A.M., the phone rings.

"How's everything going? . . . Yeah, I heard about Edsel this morning. I hope it's a good move for him. . . . Any good news for me? . . . I got it. . . . That's great. It's just what I've been waiting to hear."

Farr hangs up. Sits back. A wide grin stretches across his chocolate-hued, mustachioed face. Ford has approved his request for a $30 million line of credit. "This is great," he beams. "Now, I can develop used-car superstores across the nation. Mel Farr will be *the* major player in the urban market. I feel as though my business life has just started again."

Creating New Openings

Over the years, Farr has forced himself higher and higher among the ranks of auto dealers, and will not be satisfied until he's the biggest and the best—black or white. He's pushed himself forward by selling, lobbying, hustling, acquiring.

Whatever it takes is his daily credo for getting things done.

In his football days as a running back, Farr created openings by dodging 300-pound defensive linemen to score touchdowns. He was talented, but his wins didn't come from the old fan's tale of natural ability. They came from training hard, studying the rules, sizing up the competition, and, of course, sheer force of a strong will.

His discipline made Farr a winner on the field—and in the boardroom.

The Drive to Success

It all started in 1944 when he was born in the small Southern village of Beaumont, Texas. He, like other blacks there, endured the restrictions imposed by Jim Crow. Lesser men would have been content staying in their place. Mel Farr, on the other hand, was going places.

I remember my older brother and me having to sit in the back of the bus, drink from the "colored only" water fountains, and sit in the restricted area when we went to the movies. If you were black, you were excluded. That would have kept many people from dreaming and striving. My father, on the other hand, showed us that you can carve out a life for yourself no matter what obstacles were in your path.

Miller Farr, Sr., did just that. The truck driver had a passion for automobiles, and saved enough of his earnings to launch Farr's New and Used, a car dealership, in 1960. To this day, Farr keeps his father's dealership license mounted on his office wall as a powerful reminder of the distance his family has traveled. It brings back sweet memories of the days when he, alongside his brother, Miller, Jr., cleaned cars and showed customers models on the lot as his father closed sales.

I guess that the car business has been in my blood most of my life. I gained so much knowledge about automobiles working for my father in what you would consider a backyard operation. He showed me that if you applied hard work to any task, you could get what you want. For us, a typical family outing was going to a car lot and checking out the competition's prices. We would take trips to the junkyard where we would buy cars, fix them up, and sell them for a profit.

The center of young Mel's enthusiasm about cars was his prized red-and-white 1955 Buick Special. Tooling around town in the car, he was the BMOC at all-black Herbert High, making his friends envious and attracting bobby-soxers. Farr enjoyed the attention. He always did. But, to him the car represented more than celebrity status; it symbolized the freedom and mobility that he yearned for.

So did sports. Blessed with size, speed, and agility, he became his high school's star running back. Despite this, Southern universities weren't interested in recruiting African American players no matter how well they played.

Farr's opportunities lay with black colleges as well as majority institutions on the East and West coasts. After reviewing several offers, he accepted a football scholarship to the University of California, Los Angeles.

I decided to go to UCLA because of its tradition of developing pioneers. It's where some of my heroes went to school. Jackie Robinson went there and then broke the color line in baseball. Rafer Johnson attended UCLA and was the first African American to get a gold medal in the decathlon. I believed that if I went there, I could achieve greatness, too.

Farr didn't betray that athletic legacy. He was named an all-American twice. One day, he read about football running back Jim Brown signing a $100,000 contract to play for the Cleveland Browns—one of the largest ever for an African American. He figured that he, too, could make his fortune in pro football.

In 1967, after his senior year, he joined the National Football League (NFL) draft and was the seventh pick by the Detroit Lions. At 22, he was on his way, signing a three-year $94,000 contract.

Not bad. But, in Farr's mind, not good enough.

How dare they not pick him as the No. 1 draft pick! He was going to show everyone who's the best. He would be named Rookie of the Year. And, he was going to become a millionaire doing it. Surely, his performance and star quality could translate into big bucks on—and off—the gridiron.

By the end of his first season, Farr earned a spot in the Pro Bowl and received the NFL Rookie of the Year honor. His second objective, however, was blocked.

When he went to the Lions to negotiate a fatter contract, the owners flat-out refused to bargain with him. After hiring an agent to get him lucrative commercial endorsements, he was turned down by consumer-products companies, too. His supplemental income: $500 for being named Rookie of the Year.

During his second season, he almost lost it all. In one game, the usually elusive Farr collided with the human equivalent of a Mack truck, injuring his knee. For the first time, he left the field on a stretcher.

It was Farr's wake-up call.

From my hospital bed, my thoughts were: I'm 23 years old. If I can't play football, how will I provide for my wife and two boys? If I stay in the league, then what am I going to do after football? I came to realize that there were no guarantees that I'd be able to play for several years. Football was a short career, and I would still be a young man after my playing days were over. So, I had better start making moves now to secure my family's future.

Farr began to prepare for life after the cheering stopped.

The automobile industry was a natural choice. His greatest passion, besides family and football, was cars. He already worked in the industry's capital, and his team's owner was a Ford family member and could provide access to company executives.

As an African American, I could not see being a coach in the National Football League, because there weren't any. I could see myself as an auto dealer. I gained that example from my father. I really wanted to find out how the automobile business worked. I was able to get a job at Ford. They asked me if I wanted to work in public relations for the company's racing team and make a lot of money or work in dealer development and learn the retail side of the business. I wanted something solid after football. I opted to make $200 a week in the dealer development program.

It was 1968, a time when Ford's business goals intersected with its social objectives. A year earlier, Detroit, like many urban hubs, was set ablaze during the long, hot summer of 1967. Henry Ford II watched as the city burned, and made a public vow that his company would open doors for African Americans. That same year, the company launched its first black-owned dealership.

I often got teased by my teammates. They drove around in Cadillacs, Lincolns, and Mercedes while I drove my Mustang.

They'd ask me, "Why are you working at Ford Motor

*Company for $200 a week when you are a profes-
sional athlete?"*

I'd reply, "I'm going there to steal."

*Confused, they'd ask, "You mean that you are going
to steal transmissions and engines off the line?"*

*"No," I'd say, "I'm going to steal me some knowl-
edge about the automobile industry. I'm going to learn
how to make money and be a businessman."*

*You see, most entrepreneurs want to jump into a
new business before they really spend time learning
it. I received a seven-year apprenticeship before I got
my own dealership. I learned all of the basics. I sold
cars. I worked in the body shop. I took all of the retail
classes and seminars. I got an overview of what it
takes to make a dealership work.*

During his off-season, Farr spent months scouting for
black candidates at existing Ford dealerships. He found
only five, and they couldn't meet Ford's capital requirements.

Seeking a solution, he consulted with his boss, Levi
Jackson. The two took Farr's case to top brass, and they
agreed to start a black dealer training program. Over the
next three years, the junior executive studied, alongside
other black trainees, how to manage inventory, develop
repair services, and finance customers.

The other man who showed him the ropes was John Mallon, head of the company's dealer development program.

*John Mallon was the man who helped me most as I
was coming up in the business. He'd have me exam-
ine the operations of Ford's wholly owned stores and
the liquidation of failed dealerships. There was no image more impactful than to see someone lose their
dealership. The sign with the owner's name would
come down. His inventory would be taken over. He'd
have to pass over the keys to what used to be his
store. Mallon would always tell me that it was most
important to stay liquid, make payroll, and put your
money back in the business. On every transaction,*

> *you had to establish the cost of inventory and the sell-*
> *ing price. Then, you had to figure out your selling ex-*
> *penses associated with each car in order to show a*
> *profit. In examining the books of failed dealers, [one*
> *could see that] a lot of them simply didn't do that.*
> *They were businessmen, not merchants. Merchants*
> *operate their businesses at a profit.*

Over the years, Farr worked a schedule that simply de-fied comprehension. He played football, worked in dealer development, and took night classes at the University of Detroit to complete his degree. With each season, he took more crushing blows on the football field. But he was de-termined to stay in the game long enough to earn the cash to purchase his own dealership.

When the Lions decided to trade him in 1974, Farr de-cided to hang up his cleats.

"I'm quitting the game. The game is not quitting me," he said at the time.

Competing in the Automotive Arena

Out of football, Farr wasted no time scouting for a deal-ership. Even though he had helped design the black auto dealership program, Ford executives weren't con-vinced he had the chops to go it alone. They agreed to award him a franchise only if he found an experienced partner.

He selected John Cook, a former dealer he worked with during his days in the dealer development program. Farr persuaded Cook to come back into auto retailing, and they put up $40,000 each to buy the franchise. It would be a classic division of labor: Cook would handle the books while Farr concentrated on sales. In 1975, Oak Park–based Cook-Farr Ford, Inc., opened its doors.

The former football player had a lot to prove. He knew firsthand the statistics on dealership bankruptcies, and it just wasn't in his nature to settle for second best. Despite his experience and personage, the superstar discovered that going on the offensive on the field worked against him on the lot. On occasion, Farr's hard-charging style turned customers away.

The biggest mistake that I made was that I had not learned the difference between personal pride and pride in performance. Customers would come on my lot and I would tell them the car that they should buy. My ego got in the way of the sale. After I lost a number of sales, I reviewed my technique with Mallon, and asked him what I was doing wrong. He pointed out something very simple: The customer is always right. From that point on, I started listening to my customers and asking them questions. I became focused not only on selling cars but [also on] serving their needs.

Eventually, his sales approach took hold. By 1977, Cook-Farr debuted on the B.E. 100 with gross revenues of $9.8 million.

But storm clouds brewed. The ex-gridiron star clashed with his partner. Farr wanted to attract more customers through dynamic marketing. Cook wanted to pursue a more cautious approach.

The dealership that we acquired had gone bankrupt twice. We had to start from ground zero, hiring new employees and building a customer base. It became apparent that John and I had totally different ideas of what it would take to make money. What I wanted to do in life and what John wanted to do in life were totally opposite. I had a mission. I wanted to be the best car dealer I could possibly be. He just wanted to earn a living. He really underestimated the drive of Mel Farr. I wanted to change white folks' attitude about black athletes. I felt that most believed that we could run down the football field and score a touchdown, sink baskets, or hit a ball out of the park, but when it came to business, we didn't have the aptitude. I had two strikes against me when I started—I was black and an ex-football player. I wanted to change some of the perceptions about whether blacks who played sports could run successful businesses.

In 1978, Farr bought Cook out and ran the operation as a solo act. On closer inspection of the books, Farr discovered that the dealership was in dire financial straits. On top of that, it would be rocked by one of the industry's greatest shock waves.

It was the worst of times for auto dealers. The American economy wobbled when hit by the most calamitous recession in the past 25 years. In 1979, the fall of the Shah of Iran, the Islamic revolution, and hostage crisis in that country all conspired to keep world oil prices rising. Lines formed at gas pumps and the few people buying cars were looking for fuel-stingy compact models. The Big Three auto manufacturers—General Motors, Ford, and Chrysler—had little to offer them.

African American auto dealers hit the skids. Not only were car buyers steering away from their showrooms, the franchisees had a tough time meeting "floor plan" costs, the interest they paid manufacturers for the cars held in inventory. Over the next two years, the body count mounted. In 1979, 37 black auto dealers made the B.E. 100 list. By 1980, roughly 20 percent of them were gone.

Farr's dealership looked like it was going to join the heap of casualties. Between 1978 and 1979, his new cars sales fell 30 percent, new truck sales dropped 15 percent, and used cars sales dipped 10 percent. In 1978, the 35-year-old entrepreneur's operation generated revenues of $14.6 million, making it the nation's 16th largest black-owned business. By 1980, the dealership's sales were down to $8.6 million.

It was devastating. Black dealers were in tougher shape than general dealers because we had the least staying power. With interest rates close to 20 percent and not being well capitalized, there was no relief and the end of the downturn was nowhere in sight. Man, it was a struggle—1979 was a tough year; 1980 was even tougher. I had to scramble to make sure that I

had enough money to make payroll. I was trying to op-
erate with no cash. I finally had to reduce my person-
nel from 90 employees to 38. I literally became the
sales manager, the general manager, the janitor. I had
to do it all. During the day, I would go to auctions to
buy cars and put them on my lot because I had noth-
ing new that my customers wanted to buy. I had Pin-
tos, Granadas, Fairmonts, and LTDs. These cars
burned a hell of a lot of gas and were tough to sell.
During the day, I worked hard to sell my inventory. At
night, I would change into my jeans and my sons and
I would scrub the showroom floors.

Out of options, Farr undertook another huge sales job:
convincing the federal government to support his dealership through stormy times. In 1979, things became so
dire that Congress approved legislation that guaranteed
loans of roughly $1.5 billion to bail out Chrysler. In addi-
tion, the Carter Administration made $400 million in
Small Business Administration (SBA) loans available to
automobile dealers. To make sure black franchises like
his weren't left out of the equation, Farr mobilized black
franchisees to form the Black Ford–Lincoln-Mercury
Dealers Association, which met with the automaker and
demanded that it use its clout to back ailing stores. Then,
Farr enlisted the aid of civil rights activist Jesse Jackson
and his organization, Operation PUSH, to plead their case
in Washington. The end result: He was able to borrow
$200,000 from the SBA and the same amount from Ford
Motor Credit to rev up his operation.

It was the first step in Farr's comeback.

Next, he needed bodies. He was savvy and calculating
enough to know he needed a gimmick to lure customers.
Alone one night in his dealership, he thought about the
public persona he created. He looked at his old football
jersey. With each touchdown, he had grown larger than
life, and fans were drawn to his superheroic feats. Even
though his playing days were behind him, Farr was still a
local hero—albeit a fading one. It was time to capitalize on
the image now before he became a dim memory.

Once again he became "Mel Farr, Superstar," the tag he carried on the field. In fact, that's what he renamed the dealership. To take hold, that image would have to be beamed into the homes of thousands of Detroit residents. He needed to create television spots, but didn't have the money to hire professionals. So, he became a one-man production team, writing, directing, and starring in the ads. He even filmed them with his own video camera. Dressed in a business suit and a flowing red cape, he flew over Detroit like Superman as his theme music played: "Mel Farr to the rescue. . . . Mel Farr to the rescue."

The commercials were low-budget and hokey—and a hit.

Over the next two years, the spots drove customers to his lot. In 1982, the store's annual sales bounced back to $10.6 million. A year later, his dealership grossed $14.5 million. Farr was back on track.

> *Things were so bad that I figured that I might as well go for it. Cutting costs, lobbying for loans, developing the ads—that's how I was able to survive. I decided that I was going to do anything to bring customers on this lot. A black guy in a cape was sure to get attention. I'm a black guy on TV selling autos, which you don't see very often, and, at the time, I was talking very fast. I wanted to create an urgency to my message. Also, the name Mel Farr most people remembered from the Lions. I did things that were corny and people either hated them or liked them, but they remembered them. The key was getting customers into the showroom.*
>
> *As a running back, I'd have to go through the defensive line repeatedly. I would never stop trying because, sooner or later, I knew that I would get an opening. After I got one, I was going for the touchdown. It was during those dark days that I remembered the characteristics of winners and losers that I learned playing football.*

Today, if you walk through Farr's headquarters, from the CEO's office to the repair shop, you'll see the following mission statement plastered on walls:

1. Winners visualize future success while losers rely on the past.
2. Winners cause change while losers wait to react.
3. Winners go with winners while losers rescue losers.
4. Winners focus on customers while losers sell price.
5. Winners continually improve while losers accept good enough.
If I succeed, I will be often pleased but never satisfied.

As the economy rebounded, the dealership flourished and Farr transformed his zany plugs into more elaborate spots. The commercials became so successful that the media tapped him as a spokesman for innovative sales techniques. Locals asked for his autograph—even while he was selling cars on the lot.

Once the P. T. Barnum–style razzle-dazzle worked, Farr's charge to his sales staff was simple: Don't let any customer leave the lot without buying a new car. He polished up his act from his days as a rookie dealer, and created a new standard for his salespeople to follow.

People don't buy autos from people they don't trust. The first thing that I would do is ask them a series of questions. Are you married? Do you have kids? Do you need the car for work or pleasure? Are you paying in cash or do you need financing? I wanted to help them make the right selection. In that way, I would be considered a friend. Sometimes they'd come in looking for an Escort and drive off with a Lincoln Continental. I trained all my employees to use the same technique.

As his Ford dealership became profitable, Farr branched out. He was among a pack of black dealers who began developing a complex of multiple dealerships. With bigness came economies of scale: charging off the television advertising expenses and spreading accounting costs across each franchise. Between 1986 and 1995, Farr acquired several more Ford and Lincoln-Mercury franchises, most of them located in Michigan and Ohio, and financed them through loans from banks and Ford Motor Credit.

Each acquisition had its own unique set of challenges. In 1991, his management team orchestrated an overhaul of a dealership he purchased in Fairfield, Ohio. The store's sales had slid because of its reputation for shoddy customer service and poor employee morale. In fact, the franchise had sold only 70 cars a month and lost all its service department employees. But, Farr knew the location could be a moneymaker.

He installed his older son, 25-year-old Mel, Jr., as the general manager and devised a strategy to resurrect the dying franchise. Over the next two years, he recruited new employees, who were attentive to anybody who came on the lot. They used the same type of hype to attract new customers in the predominantly white area. The difference: They hired a white actor to play the red-caped Mel Farr barking out bargains. By 1995, the dealership was selling 400 cars per month, and gained top honors from the automaker for sales and customer service.

Finding Gold in Foreign Cars

In the 1980s, Farr honed in on the growing success of Japanese cars in the United States. In his mind, he had gained enough experience and sales volume to successfully manage a foreign-car franchise. Having learned the tough lessons from the "Crash of '79," he wanted greater dealership diversification. He applied for the Toyota dealership, and was turned down flat.

The procurement of foreign-car franchises has always been difficult for black entrepreneurs. Unlike their American counterparts, Japanese manufacturers did not develop programs to recruit and train minorities. In the early 1980s, only four black dealers had been able to purchase these elusive, but lucrative, outlets. Farr said at the time:

The Nissan and Toyota dealers were making a lot of money and, hell, I wanted to make money, too. It's unfair for them to come into our community and ask us to buy their cars and we can't sell them.

To secure one of these dealerships, he'd have to apply pressure. Once again, he worked with a coalition of black dealers and civil rights organizations to make inroads. He marshaled his forces, pushing black members of the National Association of Minority Auto Dealers (NAMAD) to pry open the import field. The effort required calls once again to Jesse Jackson, who had successfully structured covenants with consumer-products and fast-food companies to reach out to black businesses. Farr even took a series of trade missions to Japan to lobby government and industry. With foreign carmakers striking accords with domestic manufacturers to make models in the United States, he argued, these companies should award franchises to blacks.

It took Farr six long years, but Toyota finally awarded him a franchise. When he opened the dealership in Bloomfield Hills, Michigan, in 1989, it was only the fifth black-owned Toyota dealership in America. Four years later, he increased his penetration into the foreign car market by purchasing Mazda and Volkswagen franchises from Autobahn Motors, a local dealership, placing his portfolio of midrange foreign models under one roof.

Steering to Diversification

Not all of Farr's acquisitions were touched by Midas. He shut down his Aurora, Colorado, Lincoln-Mercury dealership in 1986 within 30 months, because it was too far away for him to properly manage.

In May 1985, he purchased a Seven-Up bottling franchise with fellow auto dealer Al Bennet and attorney Charles Wells. Once again, Farr was a beneficiary of Jackson's efforts: Operation PUSH signed a trade agreement with Seven-Up to increase the number of minority franchises. Using a combination of personal savings, bank loans, and government funds, the three investors shelled out a total of $5.5 million to acquire the Flint, Michigan, bottling operation. Within two years, the partners sold the business when Seven-Up became resistant to their plans to expand into other territories.

It took more time to convince Farr to become involved in the gaming business. In 1996, Detroit's city fathers discovered that they could pump $2 billion into the local economy and diversify its industrial base through allowing casino gambling. Casino corporations stormed the city in an attempt to gain one of the three licenses up for grabs. Most of these companies, including MGM Grand and Circus Circus, sought Mel Farr as a partner. They felt having the successful local businessman on board would give them an edge with city hall.

Another of Farr's suitors was none other than Donald Trump. Farr turned the billionaire down three times. But Trump kept calling back.

The auto dealer finally met with Trump, who laid out his plan for their $200 million casino in the heart of Detroit.

"Mel," Trump asked, "why don't you want to be a part of the casino business?"

"Quite frankly, I don't want to be distracted from building up my automotive business. Also, I don't like being part of a large group."

"I can understand that. Our partnership would be small. Besides, it wouldn't just be a chance to be a part of the casino business, but the development of Detroit. If I get the license, I am committed to building homes and demolishing vacant buildings around schools."

Farr was impressed with Trump's reputation in the gaming industry, and believed he would be sensitive to the needs of urban residents, since he had built casinos in Atlantic City. Redevelopment would mean new customers for Farr's urban store. Even if they didn't pull it off, any partnership with The Donald would provide him with thousands of dollars of free publicity for his franchises. Farr finally said yes.

On June 20, 1997, Trump and Farr made their announcement at the opulent Fisher Theatre in downtown Detroit. Before a throng of local newspaper and television reporters, the master pitchman couldn't pass up the promotional opportunity. To punctuate their announcement, Farr draped his trademark red cape over his new partner's shoulders. The next day, the newspapers proclaimed, "The Donald Joins Superstar Mel."

Six months later, the Farr/Trump bid was rejected by Mayor Dennis Archer in favor of three others. So much for the magic of the cape.

The transaction that was more to Farr's tastes, however, brought him together with another local legend. In 1995, he teamed up with Dave Bing, the former Detroit Pistons basketball player, to create a company that would make and supply parts for the Big Three. (Bing's $183 million steel processing concern ranks fifth among B.E. industrial/service companies.)

Farr bought a 22 percent stake in Bing Manufacturing, Inc., a 17-acre plant that sits in Detroit's empowerment zone. Besides employing more than 100 people, the company received significant tax breaks for investing in an economically depressed area.

The deal was tailor-made for the two men. First, the former sports superstars had known each other for roughly 30 years. More importantly, there was a strategic fit: Bing brought his manufacturing experience while Farr had connections with Ford and other carmakers.

Bing Manufacturing serves as a perfect model for the type of partnerships that I will be involved in. I don't have to take the focus off of my primary business. It is a business that is related to my industry. And the people who run the business don't have to learn it; they know it intimately.

Targeting the Uncreditworthy

Farr's multiple franchises cushioned him from the bloodbath that car dealers suffered during the recession of 1991. Not only did Farr's company avoid shrinkage;

his dealerships grew 16 percent that year, to $106 million.

Farr's success, during good times and bad, was buoyed by a strategy full of irony: his willingness to cut deals with people with bad credit. In 1990, he set up his own finance company, Triple M Financing (named after his two sons, Mel, Jr., and Michael, and his daughter, Monet) so he could make arrangements with customers who couldn't get loans through Ford Motor Credit. Because these customers were poor risks, he beefed up his infrastructure. If a payment was two days late, his employees started calling customers. If just two more weeks passed without payment, the vehicles were repossessed.

The finance company became the catalyst for his latest corporate strategy: opening a national chain of used-car superstores. Unlike Wayne Huizenga, the entrepreneur who developed the blockbuster used-car dealership trend, Farr seeks out urban customers who have been traditionally shunned by majority operations. This market will continue to grow, he maintains, with the growth in the number of bankruptcies and the unloading of sub-prime paper, or poor-quality debt, by smaller dealers.

Farr set up his Ferndale location, which has an inventory of 500 cars priced at around $10,000, specifically to target such customers. As a service, the dealership holds seminars on credit maintenance and personal budgeting aimed at making his customers better consumers. If a vehicle needs to be repaired and the purchaser doesn't have the money to fix it, Farr rolls the repair bill into the monthly payment. As early as 1996, he spent $6 million acquiring new urban dealerships based on this model.

In September 1998, Farr made the rounds on Wall Street to securitize his car loans—issuing high-yield bonds backed by this type of debt. His $30 million line of credit from Ford Motor Credit has provided him with the liquidity to assume bad debt as well as finance future acquisitions.

I feel like the first gold miner who discovered gold. Most companies see the emerging markets overseas. I see the emerging markets in Detroit, Houston, Baltimore, and Dayton. The urban customer, whether African American, Latino, or white, needs to have cars because mass transit no longer serves them. I am going to be the one to sell them that car. I am also positioning myself as the leader of the sub-prime market. I'm going to finance credit risks. I am going to buy subprime paper from other dealers and liquidate it profitably. Dealers will pay us a premium to buy it and I will raise the interest rate on customers to build the reserves to cover it. We'll be the leaders of this market because there's no real competition.

As his father did in Beaumont, Farr will realize his dream of urban expansion with the help of his family. His brother, Miller, Jr., who also played for the Detroit Lions, manages the profitable Lincoln-Mercury franchise in Waterford, Michigan. His sister-in-law oversees human resources. And, his two sons, former pro football players Mel, Jr., and Michael, have followed in their father's footsteps not just in sports, but in automobile sales as well.

I didn't know it at the time, but my father was laying the foundation for me to go into this business. I did the same with my sons. When they were younger, they would come to my first store and play in the office. They would sit in my chair. I'd tell them to get out of my seat. I told them that they had to earn the right to sit in the chair. I didn't joke about that. You pay the cost to be the boss.

Farr's tab has long since been paid in full.

EMMA C. CHAPPELL:
UNITED BANK OF PHILADELPHIA

The People's Banker

EMMA C. CHAPPELL

Age: 55.

Birthplace: Philadelphia, Pennsylvania.

Marital Status: Divorced.

Children: Two daughters, Tracey and Verdaynea.

Education: B.S., Temple University; Graduate Degree, Stonier School at Rutgers University (banking and finance); five honorary degrees.

Entity: United Bank of Philadelphia.

Established: 1992.

Services: Banking and financial advisory services.

Assets: $108.9 million.

Mission: To be Philadelphia's premier customer service–based one-stop shop for financial products and services with a dedication to minorities and women.

Number of Employees: 80.

First Job: Clerk-photographer for Continental Bank.

Mentors: Civil rights activist Reverend Leon Sullivan; NationsBank CEO Hugh McColl.

Chappell's Basics: *Nothing in the world can take the place of persistence.*

On Strategy: *Above all else, entrepreneurs must have clarity. They must clearly define their company's mission, products, services, and strategy.*

On Sharing the Wealth: *Even though you started the company, you should not let your employees feel as if you are alone in the venture. Be clear that your success will mean their advancement.*

7

EMMA C. CHAPPELL:
UNITED BANK OF PHILADELPHIA

The People's Banker

Leadership . . . can only be [demonstrated] through example. . . . I never ask someone to do something that I wouldn't do or haven't done.

It was Emma Chappell's baby.

She conceived the idea, and bore the heavy burden of giving it life. Then, from the day she launched United Bank of Philadelphia, she nurtured it, protected it, expanded it.

It took six long, hard years.

Finally, on a clear March day, it was time to party. The bank was having a birthday. Scores of balloons in blue and white, the bank's crisp signature colors, floated throughout its interior. Television crews filled the lobby. Champagne flowed.

If anyone had earned the right to celebrate, it was Chappell. But there she was, as always: hard at work.

The short, energetic 55-year-old wears several hats— founder, booster, chair, salesperson, president, and CEO. Every few minutes or so, one of her 80 employees or 27,000 customers enters her office. In the morning, she meets with union officials about managing a significant chunk of their pension fund. Midday, she talks to a brokerage firm about how United can make inroads into government bond underwriting. Later in the afternoon, she's playing model in a photo shoot to market 26 ATMs located throughout the metropolitan area. The following morning, she'll hop on a plane to be part of President Clinton's delegation to Africa.

Sounds daunting, perhaps, but to Chappell, this is the stuff of which dreams are made. Ever the pragmatist, though, she admits it's not easy keeping the dream alive.

Probably the toughest part is trying to get everything done. You have to be able to move on a dime. [Entrepreneurs] have to learn time management skills. That means writing a list of your daily objectives and prioritizing them throughout the day. And, if you have an assistant, make sure that he or she knows your daily objectives and schedule so that you can meet your goals.

"He or she"—it's an offhand reference that shows a consideration for gender that few male CEOs have internalized. The fact that she is a rarity—black and female—in her industry, at her level, is obvious. Having begun her career in banking at age 18, she's known little else. So, unless specifically pressed to address a subject, she doesn't. Frankly, time and energies are dominated by more pressing business issues. At the same time, she has never tried to alter her natural style to suit some male mold or expectation.

Chappell doesn't bark orders; she speaks in the calm, precise tone of a seasoned college lecturer. But, her unruffled exterior masks an iron will. The worker bee has risen in the dog-eat-dog world of banking through equal parts of order, discipline, purpose, and passion. She's molded her institution through strategic relationships with a clear eye on forging a "customer-obsessed" culture that can beat out any bigger-name competitor. As a result, the company that Chappell built is one of the nation's largest black-owned banks, with assets of $108 million and deposits of $99 million.

Her accessibility, empathy, and loyalty to her staff and the community she serves have earned her the title "The People's Banker." The moniker smacks of a marketer's genius, but it's actually well-deserved.

[Entrepreneurs] need to demonstrate leadership. This can only be accomplished through example. Person-

ally, I never ask someone to do something that I wouldn't do or haven't done. You must keep on top of your competitive environment and share information with your staff. Even though you started the company, you should not let your employees feel as if you are alone in the venture. Be clear that your success will mean their advancement.

The creed Chappell lives by—and regularly relates to others—is adopted from President Calvin Coolidge:

Nothing in the world can take the place of persistence. Talent will not; nothing is more common than unsuccessful people with talent. Genius will not; unrewarded genius is almost a proverb. Education will not; the world is full of educated derelicts. Persistence and determination are omnipotent.

One need only hear the story of her bank to understand why Chappell so firmly believes this.

Lesson #1: Always Be Receptive to New Opportunities

Born in 1943, Chappell has always called Philadelphia home. Growing up in West Philly, a black working-class neighborhood, she displayed her smarts early on, making A's and a few B's all through school. Her grades held even through a period of heartbreak; when she was 14, her mother died of complications due to sugar diabetes. Her father, George, a chef at Horn & Hardart Restaurant, raised her.

At first, young Emma wanted to be a nurse. The sight of her mother's diminishing life and vitality was a memory that she just couldn't shake. But her pastor, Reverend Leon Sullivan of Zion Baptist Church—who would later gain prominence from his protests of apartheid in South Africa—would change that course.

In 1959, as Chappell prepared to graduate from high school, Sullivan began counseling her about the future and encouraged her to take an aptitude test. Chappell aced the math section.

"I have just the job for you," Sullivan said, after reviewing her scores. "You should work in a bank."

A banking career had never crossed her mind. "Why?" she asked.

"One, you have the aptitude," he replied. "More importantly, we need more [African American] bankers who can make an impact in our communities."

The conversation went just that way, Chappell recalls. And, ever eager to please those whom she admired, Chappell accepted his assertions without question or pause.

Sullivan's connections helped Chappell land a $45-a-week entry-level position at Continental Bank, where she made copies of checks as a clerk-photographer part-time while attending college full-time. She diligently completed her assignments, but set her sights on another position early on: "I wanted to handle the money."

She closely watched the bank tellers perform their duties, taking mental notes. When the day came that the bank needed a replacement teller, Chappell volunteered and immediately excelled.

It would be a pattern that she followed throughout her career: quickly succeeding in one position, then leapfrogging to the next. Over the years, she served in every position imaginable at one of the city's most prominent financial institutions—administrative assistant, branch manager, assistant treasurer, and credit specialist. Then, at the age of 34—18 years after she entered Continental as a wide-eyed teen—the wunderkind became the first black vice president in the bank's history and the first woman to hold such a position at any financial institution in Philadelphia.

The speed and uniqueness of her ascent were never lost on her.

> *I was always receptive to new opportunities in the bank. But I felt that I had to be careful of my relationships with male managers. As a woman, I didn't want my reaching out for help to be perceived as having any ulterior motives. It became very important that my promotions would be perceived as being based solely on merit.*

Also key to Chappell's rise was the work that she did outside the bank. At first, conservative Continental wasn't keen on Chappell's involvement with such organizations as the NAACP and the Southern Leadership Conference, and she eased off. Then, with the rise of government initiatives to help the poor, community involvement became an asset, so she seized on it. In 1971, she established a special program to approve business loans and extend credit to low- and moderate-income customers. Two years later, she took a leave of absence to help city officials organize the Model Cities Business and Commercial Development Corporation (known today as the Philadelphia Commercial Development Corporation), which financed economic development projects throughout the city. When she returned to the bank, in 1975, she was designated liaison officer to the Small Business Administration, dispersing $30 million in loans to businesses owned by minorities and women.

I didn't want to sit back and miss anything. I wanted to give blacks equal access to the banking system, whether they were putting money in a passbook savings account or trying to get a mortgage to buy a new home. I came to realize that the power to effect such change would come from being a bank president or starting a bank, not [from] staying at a mainstream institution or working on Wall Street.

But the long hours, especially in the early years of her career, required personal sacrifice. As a divorced single parent, she didn't have much time for raising her two daughters, Verdaynea and Tracey.

The toughest part was trying to manage my schedule and spend time with my girls. As the promotions came, I was able to get a live-in nanny, which made things much easier. As much as possible, I tried to involve them in what I was doing. In later years, their involvement became more evident with the establishment of United. Verdaynea, who went to Wharton, served on the board, and Tracey works with the community development arm of the bank.

In 1984, she took another leave to join Jesse Jackson's presidential campaign as national treasurer, with oversight of its $11 million war chest. Attending Rutgers' Stonier School of Banking part-time, she was about to complete her master's work. It was Jackson's historic run, with its focus on self-determination, that encouraged Chappell to create a hometown bank. In fact, her master's thesis, "A Banking Strategy for Minority Business Development," would serve as the blueprint.

Lesson #2: Have Clarity in Your Mission and Strategy

The venture got off to a promising start. With her impressive credentials and fat Rolodex of contacts, she organized a group of 12 African American investment bankers and business leaders to plot the founding of the bank.

Building a financial institution from scratch would take loads of capital. First, Chappell and the others ponied up $600,000 to develop a business plan and a feasibility study. To take the next step—establishing United as a state-chartered institution—they needed to raise $3 million.

Chappell put in place a strategy to gain the financing. She would approach insurance companies, corporations, and leading financial institutions. Her leverage would be the poor track record of majority banks providing loans to African American customers. Moreover, the institutions held mediocre performance ratings as measured by the Community Reinvestment Act (CRA), the 1977 federal law created to induce banks to provide credit and other services to low- and moderate-income communities.

Chappell's pitch:

> *What better way to improve your CRA performance ratings than to invest in a bank that would fully serve minorities?*

It worked. Within months, Chappell persuaded such monoliths as Mellon Bank, PNC Bank, and Corestates Financial Corporation to shell out more than $1 million.

United was on its way.

Then Chappell's world fell apart.

On October 19, 1987, the stock market plunged 508 points and wiped out as much as $500 billion in equity value on the New York Stock Exchange. Institutional investors became skittish. United's sources of financing dried up. To make matters worse, the state raised the capital requirements to $5 million.

We put all this work into trying to start United and our strategy for raising the money from institutional investors just collapsed. But we were not ready to give up. The idea came to us that we should raise the money from the black community. Such a move had not been tried for decades. I believed that if we [African Americans in Philadelphia] truly wanted our own financial institution then we had to put our money where our mouth was.

For the next three years, Chappell mounted a tireless campaign stumping for dollars. Wearing out several pairs of shoes, she canvassed different neighborhoods and pressed the flesh with black Philadelphians—blue-collar workers, professionals, and entrepreneurs—anyone who would take a few minutes to listen. At the same time, she continued to push major corporations to buy shares and sought support from city hall.

Sitting in the small office she shared with her secretary, a worn Chappell tried to figure out the best way to accumulate huge sums of cash. Finally, she had a revelation: *The best place to spread the gospel was in church.* It wasn't exactly a novel idea, but it was all she had.

She convinced local ministers to let her address their congregations, from the pulpit on Sundays and from the dais at church functions. The polished banking executive became a financial evangelist, raising the economic consciousness of the black community—and the money she needed to finance her dream.

[In] 1989, we set out to raise $6 million in capital—$1 million more than the regulatory requirement. It was a struggle, but the response was overwhelming and

gratifying. African Americans and others from all walks of life—nearly 3000 shareholders—purchased stock in United. Some had never owned stock before, but believed in our mission. Black media [newspapers and radio stations] and others provided the impetus to encourage people to support the bank. Promotional spots were given pro bono. We held "Black Bank Sunday" in many churches throughout Philadelphia where prospectuses were distributed and discussed and stock was sold to church congregants who clearly saw the need for the bank and wanted to own a piece of history . . . a history that would have a lasting economic impact on Philadelphia and our communities. We soon became known as "The People's Bank."

By April 1991, United had received $3.3 million from individual investors and another $2.7 million from 14 institutions. The Bank the People Built had cleared its first major hurdle.

Lesson #3: Acquisition Is the Quickest Route to Growth

It took another year for Chappell to get state and federal regulatory agencies to sanction the institution. In fact, just a few hours before it planned to open in 1992, United received its state bank charter, Federal Reserve membership, and Federal Deposit Insurance Corporation (FDIC) insurance.

Chappell smiles, summing up the long road to the finish line succinctly:

Drama to the very end.

Wooing the community members had a residual effect: It increased customer demand. Eager to open new accounts, a sea of depositors anxiously awaited completion of the ribbon-cutting ceremony taking place inside. When the doors opened, scores of Philly's working class rushed the tellers' stations to deposit their hard-earned dollars. Such luminaries as Mayor Edward Rendell, members of city council, and Jesse Jackson were present, singing Chappell's praises and hailing the bank's arrival as "a catalyst for black business development."

One thing was for sure: The turnout validated Chappell's five-year campaign. It was clearly her field of dreams: She built it and they came.

Chappell's strategy was clear. The bank would start out conservatively. She'd hire a top-notch group of professional managers and advisers, but keep the chain of command short for accessibility to employees and customers.

In its first year, deposits totaled more than $18 million while the bank granted $6.3 million in loans. Most of the funds were invested primarily in government bonds and other safe, low-yielding securities. United, however, needed more cash: Its expenses—salaries, rent, and equipment—produced an operating loss that reduced its initial $6 million in capital to $4.3 million. The bank was required to maintain substantial cash reserves for operations and coverage of bad debt.

In order to grow, Chappell would have to generate income by making profitable and safe loans to individuals and businesses. But to make such transactions, United needed to expand into other communities.

The quickest route to growth was to acquire it.

Chappell's approach: scoop up branches of failed thrifts. In the late 1980s and early 1990s, the federal government sought to cure the moribund savings and loan industry. The Financial Institutions Reform, Recovery and Enforcement Act of 1989 created the Resolution Trust Corporation (RTC) as an agency charged with liquidating the assets of failed institutions. In reaction to the policy, minority lobbyists, concerned that nonblack institutions would buy and close branches in black neighborhoods, pressed the RTC to enact a preference bidding process. These auctions enabled financially sound institutions to increase capital and reserves by acquiring assets and deposits at fire sale prices.

Chappell wanted United to be one of them. To her way

of thinking, United would reap high returns with minimal risk. The key was putting in place the tactical team to shepherd them through the RTC's bureaucracy. She enlisted the services of Memphis-based Financial Consultants Inc., whose principals, M. Scott Lawyer and David C. Lensing, helped write the legislation that permitted the RTC to turn over minority bank branches that did not receive acceptable bids. Minority institutions were also given the right to bid on profitable and safe mortgages.

In the summer of 1993, United purchased two branches from Chase Federal Savings & Loan, which had $12 million in deposits, for $7777 each, and then three branches of the now defunct Home Unity Savings & Loan for another $7000.

There was a major glitch, though. Regulators were wary of letting United increase its $23 million in assets fourfold overnight. To proceed, Chappell needed a partner to bid with United.

She convinced PNC Bank to buy one of the branches. The majority institution was already a United shareholder, owning $100,000 worth of stock, and was willing to invest $750,000 more to help it meet capital requirements that would result from an increase in assets and loans. PNC benefited by allowing it to partner with a minority enterprise, one of the RTC's bidding requirements. Immediately after buying the Home Unity branches, Chappell unloaded one branch with $34.5 million in deposits. She then sold an equivalent amount in loans and deposits to First Tennessee Bank, gaining a $3 million profit from the sale.

Things were starting to come together.

Thanks to four new branches and the subsequent sale of loans, the People's Bank achieved profitability in its second year. Net income rose to $862,000, wiping out the previous year's loss. Assets totaled $77 million, a 237 percent increase over year-end 1992. Capital climbed from $4.3 million to $6.3 million, with a capital-to-asset ratio of 7.75 percent. United was so successful that the state's secretary of banking took note of its place as "one of the few [banks] to be profitable in such a short period of time."

The euphoria, however, would not last.

Lesson #4: Learn from Your Mistakes

Chappell wanted to stay the course. The acquisition of branches bolstered the institution's asset base and secured the bank while she refined its long-term strategy.

But she didn't anticipate the ire of a community. The purchase of Ukrainian Federal Savings & Loan became a hard business lesson. She believed United could duplicate its previous success through another takeover. But, the Ukrainian community didn't want intruders invading their turf.

> *When we started the bank, we said many times that the color we recognized was green. Our bank encouraged deposits, loans, and capital investment from all people. Because our mission demands a sensitivity to the special needs of African Americans, Hispanics, and women, we anticipated that those groups would constitute the bulk of our customers. They [were not intended] to be our exclusive customers.*
>
> *When we bought the Ukrainian branch, we entered into a unique situation. It was a tight-knit community where people were used to doing business with one another. They didn't know us and, when we acquired the branch, they made it known that they didn't want us to take over the institution. We thought that we could correct the situation by creating a joint venture with a Ukrainian-owned institution, First Security Bank in Chicago. It didn't work. The joint venture did not pacify that community. They were upset that we were taking their branch away. They lined up on Friday, the day that we took over. Within two weeks, the deposits dropped from $20 million to $3 million. We had to shut [it] down or the rest of United would have suffered.*
>
> *If I had to do it over again, I would not have engaged in that transaction. We didn't know the customer base. It was not worth the risk.*

To make matters worse, United was also entitled to $22 million in loans from the branch, but the RTC changed the pricing structure from 94 cents on the dollar to 99.25 cents. The bank was unable to purchase debt at that price, because it didn't have the reserves necessary to fund potential loan losses.

Chappell wasn't willing to roll over and play dead—not even for the federal government. Outraged that the RTC had treated United unfairly, she sued to gain the accrued interest on the loan portfolio. In 1996 she won, receiving $90,000 for her institution in a settlement.

Following the Ukrainian fiasco, the bank needed capital quickly. State banking laws required that United's total capital stand at 10 percent of its assets because it was a new bank. At the time, it had $77 million in assets and just $6.3 million in capital.

It was Chappell's intention to grow United's asset base to more than $100 million. To do this, she needed to raise an additional $3.7 million, and began targeting investors for another offering of common and preferred stock. She focused once again on area banks, businesses, and individuals, including current shareholders. By 1995, her second offering yielded enough funds to meet the capital requirements.

United's greatest strength was that it wasn't saddled with a bunch of nonperforming loans. Its bread and butter was tied to residential mortgage loans, which comprised $49.6 million, or 78 percent, of its portfolio. Commercial, real estate, and consumer loans constituted a total of $14.7 million. The bank's loan-loss provisions—money put aside to cover debt gone sour—grew from $191,000 to $726,000 between 1992 and 1994. Out of $63.7 million in loans, fewer than 1 percent were delinquent.

Lesson #5: Don't Just Be Service-Oriented. Be Service-Obsessed!

United had been in a difficult spot, not uncommon to small, start-up banks. It didn't have the capacity to handle high-risk loans and, as a result, become extremely profitable. Chappell needed to increase the bank's deposit level in order to develop operating economies of scale and income to cover operations.

Although United would book losses over the next two years, the People's Banker had a two-year plan to dramatically improve customer service and cost containment. She approached the task in her usual methodical manner. For starters, she formed a holding company that could develop more aggressive revenue-generating subsidiaries and investment products without hurting the bank's balance sheet. Her goal: to make the company a one-stop shop for financial products and services by the year 2000.

Chappell's mandate was simple. United would develop a customer-obsessed culture by making service the responsibility of all employees, from the security guard to the chairman. The program was ambitious and it required more of Chappell's time. But it was worthwhile, since, after all, she was taking care of not just customers but shareholders.

My customers [wanted] the personal touch of going in and being able to talk to the bank president or senior officers. People can call up and speak to me directly. I know many of my customers by name because I attend the same church that they do or their children attend school with children of the people on my staff. In some cases, we introduced ourselves to potential customers the old-fashioned way—by going from door to door.

Despite its soft, personalized touch with existing customers, United became more aggressive in going after new customers and more business. The marketing department launched cable television spots that hawked the bank's services and products, including its free checking accounts and new secured Visa card. The ads worked: The bank has 1900 secured cardholders with $800,000 of credit card loans.

Over time, the People's Bank transformed into Philly's financial classroom. United customers learned about account management and credit through financial seminars and workshops at local churches. First-time home buyers were counseled through the process at its newly created

Mortgage Center. And 2000 students were introduced to money management through the Passport 2000 program. In fact, as a means of developing lifelong customers, United established a student savings program with area elementary schools.

At the same time, Chappell attacked costs with a vengeance by implementing "cost center accounting," which required each department and branch to be accountable for managing and monitoring expenditures.

As she battened down the hatches, Chappell brought more patrons into the bank. Interest income started to grow with the expansion of the loan portfolio. The loan-to-deposit ratio increased to 75 percent. (The breakdown of United's $69 million loan portfolio: 50 percent in mortgages, 30 percent in commercial loans, and 20 percent in consumer debt.) Every day, Chappell was proving that it is possible to do well while doing good. The bank originated $10 million in student loans with a large percentage of such loans made to minority students enrolled at historically black colleges. And its financing of local businesses created 1300 new jobs.

In 1997, Chappell's customer service obsession led United to gain certification as a Community Development Financial Institution (CDFI) by the U.S. Treasury. It was the first bank in the Philadelphia area to receive such a designation. In a highly selective national competition, the U.S. Treasury also awarded the bank a $500,000 grant to establish Philadelphia United, a nonprofit corporation to offer training programs and loans aimed at revitalizing distressed communities. The University of Pennsylvania, in joint partnership with the bank, committed $500,000 in matching funds.

Chappell maintained the bank's close church ties, forming an alliance with First District African Methodist Episcopalian Church, one of the city's oldest, to provide banking services for its members. The positive impact of these actions resulted in the Philadelphia Federal Reserve giving United outstanding CRA ratings for three consecutive years.

Chappell was ready for the next phase.

Lesson #6: Stick to Your Mission; Develop Your Natural Strengths

As the bank grew, so did her daughters, and Chappell happily made it a family affair. Her daughter Verdaynea, a Wharton graduate, serves on the board, while Tracey heads the CDFI.

My daughters saw the challenges of starting this bank and they were with me every step of the way. I wanted them to be involved in a significant way because they knew the hurdles that I had to clear.

It seems that each day, Chappell reaches a bit higher. Her latest goal is to boost United's asset base to $500 million over the next few years. Though growth through acquisition proved the industry's experiential equivalent of a roller-coaster ride (exhilarating one moment, nauseating the next), its highs have outshined the lows, and so Chappell has not abandoned that strategy. Instead of pursuing failed branches, however, she now identifies healthy leftovers from merged institutions.

I think that these mega-mergers will present real opportunities for United. Like the RTC auctions, these transactions will give us the opportunity to expand assets, capital, and coverage since antitrust laws limit the number of branches that can be held by merged institutions. We know they will probably discard their urban branches. We are currently discussing with Corestates and First Union about taking over some of their existing branches in southern New Jersey and Delaware. Secondly, I believe that we can compete with the larger institutions from a service standpoint. I believe that this era of mega-mergers brings with it a depersonalization of customers.

Another arrow in Chappell's quiver is strategic relationships. Back in 1995, she persuaded NationsBank to make a $300,000 investment to shore up United's deposit base and strengthen its balance sheet. Not only did she gain an investor; she also gained an invaluable mentor when she took the opportunity to pick the brain of the institution's CEO, Hugh McColl. The straight-shooting, down-to-earth dealmeister counseled her on building up United's capital structure and adjusting the management team's strategic approach. For example, McColl gave Chappell the idea to attract large corporate customers by offering "sweep" accounts—transferring funds out of non-interest-bearing accounts and investing them overnight at high interest rates. Other aspects of these talks were incorporated into the company's strategic plan.

In recent years, the building of relationships like these has led to the expansion of United's ATM network in outlets of the Rite Aid drugstore chain and Marriott Hotels, as well as a deal with American Express Financial Advisory Services to help customers structure retirement plans and develop their investment portfolios, creating what she calls "our own in-house trust department."

The latest such development has been the partnership with FISI-Madison Inc., the largest financial institution marketing organization in the country. The outfit will train the United team on how they can secure and retain clients. Chappell expects to expand the deposit base by some 400 accounts per month.

Order. Discipline. Purpose. Passion. These are the weapons that have brought Chappell this far. These are the strengths she will harness to take United to the next millennium.

8

HERMAN J. RUSSELL:
H. J. RUSSELL & COMPANY

The Builder

HERMAN J. RUSSELL

Age: 67.

Birthplace: Atlanta, Georgia.

Marital Status: Married to Oteila Russell for 42 years.

Children: One daughter, Donata Major, 39; two sons, H. Jerome, 35, and Michael, 33.

Education: B.S., Tuskegee Institute.

Entity: H. J. Russell & Company.

Established: 1952.

Services: Construction, property management, real estate development, and airport concessions.

Annual Sales: $170 million.

Mission: To develop an international powerhouse in the construction business.

Number of Employees: 1862.

First Job: Shoe-shine boy.

First Career Move: Apprentice plasterer for his father's company.

Heroes: His father, Rogers Russell.

Russell's Basics: *Be true to yourself. Be punctual. Work hard. Master the art of saving a dollar.*

On Strategy: *If a job looked like it would take more than my company could handle, I would turn it down. I believe in controlled growth.*

On the Perils of Youth: *Young entrepreneurs today . . . want everything now. You have to have patience to stay in the game for the long haul.*

HERMAN J. RUSSELL:
H. J. RUSSELL & COMPANY

The Builder

How I operated in my life was how I ran my company. I
budgeted for everything. I didn't leave anything to chance.

Brick and mortar is Herman Russell's life.

He's turned on by fabricating new structures, providing
shelter for families and industry. His fervent pursuit of
that high led him to sculpt much of Atlanta's cityscape,
from low-rise, low-rent housing and halls of education to
the shape-shifting skyscrapers that pierce the Georgia
skies. Before he was 40, H. J. Russell's mark was already
literally set in stone.

In the process, he also built a great personal fortune,
and proved to be just as deft at managing money as he was
at laying down concrete for a foundation. A millionaire before he was 40, he could do almost anything with a dollar
bill—except lose it. Even at a time when black folk in the
South were treated like second-class citizens, Russell
found a way to get money out of first-class institutions.

All it took was courage—and a plan.

In 1955 Atlanta, it was damn near impossible for a
black man to get a business loan from a white bank. It
just didn't happen in Jim Crow's South.

But Russell, all of 24, was about to do what he'd become
known for: alter the landscape, this time, of an industry.

Determined to grow his fledgling construction business, he decided that it was time for him to take out a

loan to develop a series of duplex rental properties. A world-class penny-pincher, he'd already saved $3000, but he needed $12,000 more to purchase land, raw material, and manpower. The institution where Russell sought funds was a leader in the area: Home Federal Savings & Loan Association.

The lanky entrepreneur was known to be serious, but was not considered a rabble-rouser. He needed money. Home Federal was the place to get it. It was just that simple.

Wearing his best suit and carrying a briefcase, he walked into the bank. He could feel stares from customers and employees as he moved toward the loan desk.

"May I help you?" said an assistant, obviously taken aback by her customer.

"I came here to apply for a business loan," said Russell, his nervousness edging each of his words.

"Have a seat."

Russell looked around as he waited for a response. Not many blacks had deposited money into Home Federal; now he wanted to take money out of it.

Within a few minutes he was greeted by a loan officer, who, while surprised to see the young black man, would listen to his spiel—even if he was probably going to turn him down.

Russell explained to the loan officer that he needed money to expand, and then pulled a business plan, blueprints, financial statements, and other documents from his briefcase.

The loan officer was stunned. He had never reviewed such orderly books.

"I'll be right back," he said. "I want to talk to the president of the bank."

More waiting. Russell wondered, *Am I really going to get a loan from this place or am I just wasting my time?*

A few minutes later, Russell was ushered into the plush, cavernous office of Don Hollowell, the bank's president.

"Well, I hear that you want a loan."

Russell didn't know quite how to size up the banker.

"Thank you for seeing me," he said in his polite but resolute manner. "I have a construction business and I would like to expand it."

"Well, just how long have you been in the building trade?"

Russell once again recounted his story. He told the banker about how he had worked with his father, a plasterer by trade, and how he saved up years of earnings to buy his first tract of land. The banker listened as he surveyed the documents spread out on the desk.

After the presentation, the banker said, "We usually don't give loans to new businesses." He added, "We haven't loaned money to Negro businesses."

Russell's heart sank.

Hollowell continued, "But I tell you what. I like what you presented here. I will call you in a couple of days."

Russell had no idea what was going to happen next. He was relieved that he hadn't been turned down cold. For two days, he thought about the prospect of getting the expansion capital. If he didn't get the loan, it would mean that he would just continue to scrimp and save to develop another property. His company would creep along at best.

Two days later, he got the call that would change everything. The bank president had approved his loan.

> *I was elated. With the additional money, I was able to build more homes and expand the business. I made sure that every single loan payment was made on time. But the greatest benefit was the relationship that I was able to develop. [Hollowell] used to talk to me about how to expand my construction business as well as other ventures that I should [invest in]. At one point, he was responsible for me going into retail and liquor distribution. His advice was invaluable.*

Lesson #1: Get Your Hands Dirty

Russell scored that coup more than 40 years ago. And, as he built more and more elaborate structures, he mastered another trade: constructing deals and forging relationships. As the New South emerged—with Atlanta leading the charge—Russell had a hand in its reinvention. Beyond actually putting a new face on Southern cities, he would touch the worlds of commerce, civil rights, and politics as he achieved his ascent.

He made his money by literally getting his hands dirty, working with slate, rock, and concrete. All of the naysayers, know-it-alls, and bigots who ever tried to discouraged him he'd silence with hard work, drive, and guts. His greatest creation: H. J. Russell & Company, which has been among the nation's top black-owned businesses since *Black Enterprise* compiled its rankings in 1973, growing from a $6 million enterprise to a $170 million empire that constructs homes; develops real estate; manages properties; and handles concessions in airports throughout the nation. And, over the years, its chairman, a native son of Atlanta, has also dabbled in such diverse businesses as a beverage distributorship, a grocery store, a newspaper, radio stations and, even, professional sports.

Russell is a shining beacon in the city's black community. Shunning the downtown business district, he continues to operate in a two-story brick building on the predominantly black South Side, one of the city's most economically depressed communities. His structures touch every aspect of the builder's life, from his penthouse in the Parc Vue condominium complex—a 16-story high-rise he built—to the low-income housing he's developed on an empty lot across the street from his corporate headquarters.

To keep it all running smoothly, Russell has shrewdly organized his company into several divisions: housing and property management; construction; engineering management; development services; and regional offices in Baltimore, Detroit, and Birmingham, Alabama. His sons, H. Jerome and Michael, preside over the two key revenue-generating divisions while his daughter, Donata Major, oversees airport concessions. Now, he's positioning them to take the reins of the enterprise while moving H. J. Russell & Company (HJR) into international territory.

Lesson #2: Use Every Tool You've Got

A balding man of 67, Russell has an unassuming, humble quality. Because of an inherited speech impediment, he often leaves the last syllable or letter off words, already spoken in a thick Southern drawl. The combination makes it difficult for some first-time listeners to understand him. But, observers have said that he uses it as a tool in business dealings. Those who underestimate him quickly discover, once the ink dries on a contract, that he has gotten the better part of the deal.

He is legendary in business circles for his miserly ways, wringing the last micro-cent out of a dollar. A knowing smile spreads across his face at the mere mention of this reputed trait. He doesn't believe in grand, ostentatious gestures and is the first to say so. Unlike many of his CEO counterparts, he tools around in a Ford Navigator instead of the chauffeur-driven limousine he can clearly afford. Although his net worth has been estimated at between $40 million and $100 million, he rides coach on airplanes, eats lunch at Wendy's, and picks pennies off the ground with pride. It has been this attention to the almighty buck, some say, that has kept his company out of harm's way for more than four decades.

When I was a kid, I learned the value of a dollar. [Starting out in business], I would religiously save anywhere between 10 percent to 40 percent of my earnings. Even after I made my first million, I would not part with my old pickup truck. That's what I would drive to work as well as cocktail parties. Sometimes, it would drive my wife crazy. But how I operated in my life was how I ran my company. I budgeted for everything. I didn't leave anything to chance. If a job looked like it would take more than my company could handle, I would turn it down. I believe in controlled growth. That's one of the big problems with young entrepreneurs today. They want everything now. You have to have patience to stay in the game for the long haul.

Russell's thriftiness is a holdover from his parents, Rogers and Maggie, who raised eight children—Herman was the youngest—in the Depression era. The elder Russell was a devotee of Booker T. Washington, the former slave turned world-renowned educator who urged African Americans to "pull themselves up by their own bootstraps." Rogers Russell, a second-generation plasterer, took this philosophy of self-reliance to heart, instilling it in his large clan.

At eight, young Herman started to earn his keep, first shining shoes in downtown Atlanta and then delivering newspapers. He contributed a portion of his weekly earnings to the household and saved the rest. Rogers took his son under his wing by age 11, teaching Herman the plastering trade as his father had taught him. Within a year, Herman was considered one of the best plasterers around.

> *My father was the greatest role model to me. He taught me some of the basic fundamentals: to always be true to yourself; to be punctual; and the art of saving a dollar. My father believed in land and that rubbed off on me. He said own the land and the property on the land and you'll never go wanting. He made a believer out of me when it came to real estate. It's hard for me to give a property up once I get it.*

In fact, Russell cut his first real estate deal when he was just 15. It was the mid-1940s, G.I.s were returning home from World War II, and the high school sophomore took note of the increased demand for housing.

> *I found a small piece of land on the South Side that was being sold for $125. That was a lot of money in those days, but I had saved enough to pay the back taxes. In my spare time, I began building a duplex on the site. I used the money that I made from my plastering jobs to finance it. After I graduated from high school, I attended Tuskegee Institute [the first year paid with my savings], where I was studying building*

and construction. During the summers, I would return to Atlanta and continue to work on the duplex. When it was completed, I used the rent to pay for college. The project took years to complete. The experience taught me to establish a budget for a building project, negotiate the price of materials, and, most of all, [have] patience. I held on to that property until I sold it in 1987.

Lesson #3: Build Your Company Brick by Brick— and Never Miss a Payroll

After he graduated from college in 1953, Russell continued to look for other deals as he worked in the family business. He was still living at home, and still working side-by-side with his father.

In 1957, the Russell household and business was rocked by tragedy. The family patriarch—and foundation—suddenly died. It was an emotional blow for Russell, who not only lost a father, but his hero and mentor. He took the helm of Russell Plastering Company—a basement operation that grossed $15,000 a year—vowing to expand it as a tribute to his father. Since blacks were restricted from heavy construction projects, Russell expanded the company through small-scale residential developments. He steadily moved from duplexes to erecting four- and eight-unit apartment buildings.

The key to Russell's fortune was that, unlike other construction firms, he didn't sell the residential developments that he built. He formed Paradise Management Inc., an apartment management firm, in 1959, before such operations became big business. He then started taking the advice of his banker friend and diversifying his business interests, launching a grocery store and then a liquor distributorship.

But his heart—and goals—were in his core business: construction. Residential properties were bringing in enough to support his family, and he was able to get a job here and there at one of the local black colleges, but he wanted more. Russell aspired to what was then unthinkable for a black man: He wanted to build skyscrapers. Despite years of demonstrated prowess, his company, like other black contractors, was shut out of the bidding process as well as subcontracting opportunities.

> *I had to deal with racism. But I wouldn't let it discourage me or use it as an excuse. I just kept on bidding for jobs. Despite the hardships, I knew that I had to be the best on the projects that my company worked on. I was getting myself ready for the bigger jobs. If I was going to move my company to the next step, then I had to demonstrate excellence.*

HJR's growth accelerated in the 1960s during the tenure of Mayor Ivan Allen, Jr., considered by many to be fair to blacks during the turbulent civil rights era. Government expansion of financing aid for residential construction opened the door for Russell to find new capital for his development projects. As his reputation and Rolodex of influential contacts grew, he began to snare an increasing number of construction contracts. Despite his success, with each new job he continued his rigid process of developing a tight budget, hiring manpower, and buying materials as he needed them.

> *I developed four rules for success in business: be honest; work hard; equip yourself for the job; and control the growth of your company. I never missed a payroll. We had challenges in getting business, but the company was never in jeopardy because we didn't have enough cash reserves. I used the lean times during the Depression as my guide.*

As he stayed focused on his business, Russell didn't remove himself from participating in the Civil Rights Movement. In a decade of pressures, protests, and marches, he allied himself with many of its leaders.

Vernon Jordan, the lawyer who served as a shield for future journalist Charlayne Hunter-Gault when she became the first black to attend the University of Georgia, was one of his junior high school classmates. (Jordan would eventually become executive director of the National Urban League, a top adviser to President Bill Clinton, and a member of Russell's board.) Civil rights leader Martin Luther King, Jr., was a regular visitor to the Russell household and frequently took dips in the family's pool.

Russell didn't join the freedom rides or the marches. He wasn't sprayed with fire hoses or attacked by police dogs. But he played just as critical a role: He helped finance the Civil Rights Movement.

> *Back in those days, my home was one of the places used as a meeting place for civil rights and political strategy meetings. Vernon Jordan would say to me, "Herman, we need you to be available to post bond if we are arrested." I was one of a number of black businessmen in the South who played that role during the Civil Rights Movement.*

Lesson #4: Manage from Within the Trenches

The Civil Rights Act of 1964 and the Voting Rights Act of 1965 sparked more business opportunities. Still an outsider when it came to large commercial projects, Russell was determined to find his place in that world. He was patient, gaining credentials and experience job by job, brick by brick.

Finally, he got his chance. In 1967, he placed the winning bid to handle the fireproofing and wetwall work on the Equitable Life Assurance Building, slated to be the tallest structure in downtown Atlanta. It was a triumph. *His* triumph. Up to that point, no black firm had ever worked on a project of that magnitude. H. J. Russell & Company was on the move.

> *I made the lowest bid and I got the job. I was so excited. It was the type of work that I spent 15 years building up the company to handle. As we were about to start, I got a call from E. L. Thompson, a large contractor who had heard about us getting the job.*
>
> *He said, "Herman, I think that you made a big mis-*

> take. I like you and I don't want to see you go broke.
> Why don't you let us handle this contract for you?"
> I told him that we could handle it. I can tell you that
> phone call planted a seed of doubt. I was trying to fig-
> ure out what he could have been talking about. Did I
> overshoot? I couldn't sleep. I checked and double-
> checked my figures.
> I had a crew of 25 men. We were quick and thor-
> ough. After a quarter of the job was completed, the
> building caught on fire. If it hadn't been for our fire-
> proofing work, the building would have burned down.
> We finished our portion of the job on time and on bud-
> get. I never doubted one of my bids [again], and we
> gained a lot of respect for our work.

During the 1970s, Russell developed a three-pronged
strategy to move HJR forward: Create access through the
political process, conservatively structure bids on jobs so
as not to drain the company's coffers, and build on the
company's reputation.

By far, the biggest boost to Russell's ability to gain access
to private and public construction projects came in 1973,
when Maynard Jackson was elected Atlanta's first black
mayor. Just as he did during the Civil Rights Movement,
the 42-year-old Russell would handle the money, serving
as Jackson's campaign finance director—a role he would
repeat during Jackson's reelection bid four years later.

Jackson's election would prove fortuitous. The Jackson
administration forced contractors to include black partners and workers, establishing a city ordinance that required majority firms to guarantee African American
firms 25 percent of the total cost of contracts on some of
the city's biggest building projects.

Russell helped replicate the model in such cities as Birmingham, Alabama, and Washington, D.C., where the presence of black mayors ensured that minorities finally got an
equal shot at government contracts. His critics claimed that
HJR's expansion stemmed from so-called sweet deals, political plums derived from his many campaign contributions.
But his involvement went beyond the local level. He raised

money for Andrew Young's congressional campaign in 1974 and Jimmy Carter's presidential bid in 1976. The fact is, Russell was playing the same political game as the majority companies had been winning for decades. His access and civic involvement made him powerful corporate allies like Donald Keough, the president of the Coca-Cola Company. By the late 1970s, Russell was sought after as one of Atlanta's leading subcontractors and joint venture partners, involved in constructing some of the city's most impressive skyscrapers. The company participated in such projects as the $18 million construction of parking decks at the Hartsfeld International Airport; the $115 million Georgia Pacific Officer Tower, the second tallest building in the city; and the Metro Atlanta Rapid Transit (MARTA) system.

But significant challenges were ever-present. One of the biggest was combating white contractors that used black firms to get government contracts and then relegated them to second-class status. The other threat was front companies—scam operations in which a minority is hired as a contractor or owner of a business.

A joint venture is like a marriage. You have to live with the person until the venture is completed. With some, I had to bring more to the table than they did and some white companies wanted [me] to front for them. If we were just a front, we would never have been able to compete. I always insisted not only that we pick up our equal part in the proceedings, but that we have black people in key positions where they [could] learn.

Within a decade, H. J. Russell & Company moved from a joint venture partner to lead contractor—sometimes bringing in white firms as subcontractors on jobs. In fact, by the 1980s, HJR became so big that it wasn't eligible to bid on many of the set-aside opportunities that Russell had created. Because of its solid asset base and strong track record, it didn't suffer from a problem that plagued many other minority companies: bonding, or convincing surety companies to provide financial guarantees that work would be completed on time.

By 1983, he consolidated his businesses under one corporation. In fact, HJR's green-and-gold logo, an umbrella formed from the initials, reflects that structural change. As a result, in 1984, Russell's company became the nation's second largest black-owned business, grossing $103.8 million and employing 500 workers. It was just $500,000 shy of displacing the then No. 1 concern on the B.E. 100: Motown Industries.

The 1980s continued to be HJR's boom times. Russell owned an estimated 3500 rental units in 18 cities in Georgia. He formed a real estate development company in 1985 that built a $16 million luxury condominium complex near downtown Atlanta, one of the fastest-selling in the Southeast.

All of Russell's ventures were to feed his need to grow larger and larger. Increasing cash flow meant he could created a Goliath capable of underbidding his competitors on projects. Next to construction and real estate development, the sector in which Russell made his most significant investment was the food and beverage industry. He had proved that he could make money by providing for consumers' basic needs—shelter and sustenance.

Not all of his investments were golden, though. On advice from his banker, Russell acquired a 10 percent stake in the Atlanta Hawks basketball sports franchise. Although the team lost money, he used his skybox to entertain clients and the investment as a tax write-off.

But that was a rarity. His diversification into food grew into Concessions International, a $50 million company that operates snack shops, restaurants, and bars at major airports in Los Angeles, Chicago, Dallas/Fort Worth, Louisville, and Seattle. As in his approach to building residences, this was a natural extension of his involvement in airport construction. Only here, where he wasn't allowed to own a piece of the airport, he would at least make money from leased space. Today, his daughter, Donata Major, oversees the operation.

Russell also moved into beverage distribution. The division—City Beverage Company—distributes such popular beer brands as Stroh's, Coors, and Beck's to stores throughout southern metropolitan Atlanta. Distribution served the same value as franchises: he could sell branded products without doling out great sums of money for marketing. As a result, City Beverage grew into a $20 million operation. Russell placed his elder son, H. Jerome, at the helm of the division as a way of indoctrinating him into the family business. Russell was carrying on the tradition started by his father.

I wanted to get my children involved in the business at a young age. By the age of seven, my kids cleaned up the yards of my residential properties. There wasn't a Sunday that I wouldn't take the entire family to make spot inspections of apartment complexes after church. I was fortunate to have an understanding and loving wife who knew the sacrifices that we all had to make to get to where we wanted to be.

Despite his vast operations, Russell maintains his grip on the pulse of the company. Working 14-hour days, he still makes surprise visits at each of his divisions and properties, making sure that employees are courteous and that they wear their neat, starched white-and-green uniforms. He believes in complete access: His home phone number is still listed and he regularly takes calls from tenants and workers alike.

When you look at employees, you have to learn to read them. Anybody can give you a lovely resume, but I look for signs of leadership. Performance is the proof of the pudding. At the same time, I manage by walking around and getting involved. I never feel that I am too big to roll up my sleeves and get in the trenches with other employees.

Lesson #5: Excellence Is the Best Revenge

In January 1989, black contractors faced their greatest threat when the Supreme Court decided that municipal set-aside programs were unconstitutional. The action swept away affirmative action programs in 36 states and 200 cities. Its negative effects still ripple through the industry. In 1988, 23 construction firms made up 9.4 percent, or $389.2 million, of the B.E. 100s' revenues. By 1998, there were only four contractors left, comprising $2.2 percent, or $239.4 million, of revenues. HJR made up 36.4 percent of total sales of B.E. construction firms in 1988 versus 64 percent of the total revenues in 1998.

HJR has not been significantly affected by the ruling because it had grown large enough to be insulated. But the ruling has made it a challenge to find small black subcontractors.

> *With [fewer] programs to help minority contractors, not as many black-owned businesses are working today. What has made the situation worse is that there's a generation in which the trades were not emphasized— just white-collar jobs. As a result you don't see the development of [construction] jobs or new companies. You have to realize that the trades made black white-collar workers possible. We need to bring more blacks into the trades so that they can realize these opportunities. I am fearful that you will only see a handful of black contractors in the future, and that pool will not be replenished.*

That's why Russell makes it a point to have joint ventures with fledgling African American firms. This emphasis was evident in his involvement in the 1996 Olympics.

Back in 1990, it was announced that Atlanta had beaten out Athens, Greece, for the 1996 games. As soon as the decision was made, legions of African American firms lobbied hard for the contracts. To ensure that African Americans had entrepreneurial participation, the Atlanta Committee for the Olympic Games (ACOG) developed an equal economic opportunity program. But by 1993, not a single black firm had been awarded any prime contracts.

At best, it was a tough process for the average company. The ACOG didn't advertise upcoming contracts;

preparing a bid could cost companies as much as $25,000; and negotiating deals took months.

Moreover, the ACOG sought only companies with strong track records in their respective industries, sterling references, and solid financial footing. Even with those attributes, you needed to know how to navigate the process.

Russell, of course, fit the criteria. He had already realized that he could build a business in refurbishing old ball parks and stadiums, and developed a sports construction division in 1991. The division completed such high-profile projects as the $175 million, 1,680,000-square-foot Georgia Dome and, a few years later, began work on the $208 million Turner Field, which, in 1997, became the new home of the Atlanta Braves baseball team.

Russell went after the $209 million contract for the Centennial Olympic Stadium, the ACOG's planned centerpiece. HJR formed a joint venture with C. D. Moody Construction, another B.E. 100s company, and white-owned Beers Construction. The team submitted a company profile for ACOG's database, a requirement for all interested businesses, almost a year before bidding on the project. It took another four months for Russell to negotiate the stadium contract. Not surprisingly, he prevailed.

But winning wasn't everything. The HJR team now had to deliver—and in record time. Beating all expectations, Russell completed the 1,500,000-square-foot facility with 85,000 seats and 90 suites just before the start of the games.

Lesson #6: Prepare for the Future—Now

Russell is preparing his company to be taken over by the next generation. H. Jerome, his elder son, serves as president and chief operating officer and head of the housing and property management division. Michael, his youngest child, is the vice president overseeing the construction division. And his daughter, Donata Major, serves as president and CEO of the airport concessions operation.

To make the transition, he had brought in an outsider to get his progeny up to speed and made R. K. Seghal the company's CEO and vice chairman. Seghal, a longtime friend and associate of Indian descent, worked with Russell when HJR built bridges in Egypt during the 1970s. It was an ambitious move for Russell and, since that experience, he has focused on domestic projects. When Seghal, who operated in that role for two years, was in place, he helped the company's management focus on the international frontier once more. Such a move, Russell believes, will position the company to go public in the next millennium. Now, Russell assumes the CEO title as well as the chairmanship of the company.

> *I [briefly] brought him in so that the next generation would gain a different perspective of how to run a construction company. The growth for H. J. Russell & Company will be in the international arena. If they learn, the company will be able to make the transition. It will fuel the growth of H. J. Russell & Company for years to come.*

9

CHARLES H. JAMES III:
C. H. JAMES & SON HOLDING COMPANY, INC.

The Strategist

CHARLES H. JAMES III (AKA CHUCK)

Age: 40.

Birthplace: Charleston, West Virginia.

Marital Status: Married 15 years to Jeralyn.

Children: Three sons, C.H. IV, 12; Nelson, 11; and J. William, 5.

Education: M.B.A., Wharton School, University of Pennsylvania; B.A., Morehouse College.

Entity: C. H. James & Son Holding Company, Inc.

Established: 1883.

Headquarters: City of Industry, California.

Products and Services: Food processing and distribution.

Annual Sales: $30.9 million.

Number of Employees: 117.

First Job: Working in the warehouse of C. H. James & Company.

Heroes: *My father, my grandfather, and, especially, my great-grandfather, who started it all.*

James's Basics: *If you don't know when to change your business formula, that is when you will be replaced by your competition.*

On Racism: *When I hear black entrepreneurs complain about how hard it is today, I can't buy it. It has always been about going out and finding your niche in the marketplace, regardless of the obstacles.*

On Claiming Your Business Birthright: *You should never go straight into a family business. Build your reputation at another company first.*

Charles H. James III: C. H. James & Son Holding Company, Inc.

The Strategist

In *The Prince*, it says that a prince gains esteem through great deeds. Turning around the company would become my great deed.

Chuck James is a student of Machiavelli. Throughout his business career, his copy of *The Prince*, the centuries-old guide to gaining and keeping organizational power, has been as vital to him as his B-school credentials or his E-mail.

You see, James represents the fourth generation of his family to run C. H. James & Son Holding Company, Inc., a 116-year-old produce processor and distributor. He may have gained the business by virtue of his bloodline, but he's had to fight to keep it.

James has remade the enterprise and, in the process, taken it to unimagined heights through acquisitions, mergers, restructurings, spin-offs—anything necessary to make it thrive and grow.

At 40, he's already spent well over a decade fending off challengers and gaining allies. At times, he's had his credibility questioned: The tall, boyish-looking chief executive appears more than a decade younger. He has managed to gain respect and clout, however, through the execution of complex deals and his iron-fist-in-velvet-glove management style.

When he took over the company, it was a $2.6 million dinosaur headed for extinction. Now it is a galloping $30 million thoroughbred with three distinct units: North American Produce (NAP), that crown jewel that processes lettuce to fast-food companies and accounts for more than 50 percent of the company's sales; Pinnacle, LLC, a produce grower, shipper, and distributor; and C. H. James & Co., the wholesale food distribution operation in West Virginia, where it all started.

James is a man who believes in order and precision, whether he's driving golf balls at his country club or mapping out strategic issues at his weekly board meetings. It's that exactitude and attention to detail that feeds the company's growth.

In his business, yield—stripping the most out of the crops he buys from growers—counts for everything. Every cent he squeezes out of a head of lettuce brings him that much closer to profit. It may not be a sexy business, like entertainment or publishing, but it's profitable. That is, if you know what you're doing. And this straitlaced, fresh-faced CEO clearly does.

This warm April day, James races from one meeting to the next. Although employees enjoy a great deal of autonomy, his presence can be felt throughout the company. In the morning, he reviews a photo shoot of lettuce, onions, and carrots that will be used in a new marketing brochure. In the late afternoon, he meets with engineers to plot the redesign of the plant's production line. And, sandwiched between the sessions, he solicits price quotes on corrugated boxes used to ship produce to customers.

Clean-cut, cerebral, and textbook corporate down to his charcoal gray pinstripe suit, he operates out of his immaculate office, which is adorned with a tank of tropical fish, a Frederic Remington statuette, and McDonald's premiums. At the ready for consultation is his prized edition of *The Prince*. But his most precious memento by far is the aged black-and-white photo of his great-grandfather that rests on the credenza. An imposing figure with the glint of steely determination in his eyes, the founder stares at his great-grandson every day, almost as if he's serving as his guardian angel.

I always wanted to be in this business. All of my fore-fathers were my heroes—my father, who took the company to modern-day accounting practices; my grandfather, who rescued it from hard times; and especially, my great-grandfather, who started it all. Now, every day when I walk into my office, I have to face him. Look at him. You can tell he was bad.

Roots of an Empire

It's the trail that C. H. James blazed that drives his great-grandson. He built a business applying guts, brains, and sweat. No leveraged buyouts. No Internet. No golden parachutes.

He launched a company that became a rare example of a multigenerational business owned and controlled by an African American family—an enterprise that withstood two world wars, the Great Depression, economy-numbing recessions, and major industrial shifts.

His story starts in 1883, when the enterprising 19-year-old James created a business from bartering household wares and pictures of recently assassinated President James A. Garfield for vegetables from the cupboards of cash-poor miners and then sold the produce for cash. He was joined by his three brothers, and the trade grew from one wagon to what Chuck described in his M.B.A. thesis as "a veritable department store on wheels" that sold cotton, threads, pots, sugar, and other goods. Their business was conducted on five basic principles: dependability, integrity, a pleasing personality, humility, and human values. To this day, Chuck James has held on to those corporate virtues.

By the end of the 1890s, James became the sole proprietor when two of his brothers, Alex and Garland, died, and the third, Edward, left to start a construction company in Brazil. Instead of throwing in the towel, the entrepreneur pressed on. Twice, he outgrew his store space.

James served his predominantly white clientele of coal miners well. Despite racial epithets and other slights, he persisted, fiercely subscribing to the philosophy that "race was not and should not be an issue in business."

In 1916, he partnered with his son, E.L., a Howard University medical student, and they abandoned the retail business to become wholesalers, expanding into fresh fruits. By 1918, the concern had become the largest wholesale food operation in the state, with gross sales of more than $350,000 a year.

The company's growth transformed the elder James from a respected local merchant to a national spokesman on race and commerce. His views on black business ownership—which, in short, held that no one should let racial obstacles deter him from the vigilant pursuit of entrepreneurial success—took on a nearly evangelic fervor. In 1918, President Theodore Roosevelt wrote him a note: "I think I have spoken of you at least 100 times, pointing to you as a man who actually is by his actions and not merely by his words solving the race problem in this country."

What impressed me about my great-grandfather was that he espoused a business philosophy that is relevant to this day. The fact that he was able to overcome racism at a time when there wasn't a support system is amazing. That's why when I hear black entrepreneurs complain about how hard it is today, I can't buy it. It has always been about going out and finding your niche in the marketplace, regardless of the obstacles.

In 1926, James retired, turning over daily operations to his son. But the stock market crash three years later, followed by the Depression, sent the company spiraling into bankruptcy. Many coal companies went out of business, which, in turn, disabled C. H. James. The family's 22-room living space above the company store and wealthy lifestyle were lost. That same year, almost symbolically, the founding James died without knowing of the company's impending doom.

The resurrection of the company fell upon E.L. After the

loss of the family fortune, well over $70,000, he was forced to sell everything, including the house, to pay business debts. In 1930, he worked a series of jobs to make ends meet and kept the company afloat selling poultry and eggs. He would become the city's sole supplier of fresh eggs and eventually packaged the goods under the Blue Ribbon brand.

After 10 long years of perseverance, the business again prospered. In 1941, the concern grossed more than $200,000. With 10 employees, 4 trucks, and a warehouse, it competed against such meat-packing giants as Swift, Armour, and Wilson, which offered the less-desirable frozen products in contrast to James's fresh-dressed poultry.

In 1952, the company's poultry processing facilities went up in flames. When a city ordinance prohibited him from constructing a new building, E.L. reorganized the business from processing to distribution, becoming the largest such operation in the state. At the same time, the company began handling orders for frozen foods and canned goods in an effort to diversify. In 1961, the company operated a fleet of refrigerated trucks and used television and radio spots to sell its products. C. H. James had become a $1 million enterprise. Always haunted by the specter of financial ruin, E.L. made changes slowly—particularly those that required capital—and remained stubbornly in control of the business for the rest of his life.

E.L. was one of the real heroes of our family business. If it were not for him, our legacy would have died with the founder. Each generation has used the previous one to fuel them. No one wanted to have the company die on their watch. Each generation worked hard to preserve the legacy for the next.

When the 74-year-old patriarch died in a car crash, the business passed to his son, C. H. James II, who had started as a salesman in 1956. After years of pushing his father to modernize, C.H. II quickly put his Wharton business education to work, introducing accrual accounting, computerized purchasing, and inventory-control systems. He steered the business to serve local schools, hospitals, and restaurants throughout a 10-county region in West Virginia, Ohio, and Kentucky. But, as the company prospered and he grew older, C.H. II became a carbon copy of his father—hands-on and hard-nosed. He double-checked the work of accountants and buyers and summarily fired truckers suspected of cheating the company.

In 1976, as Chuck James prepared to enter college, his father's business was thriving. With sales of $4 million a year, it was listed among the largest black businesses in the nation. But that was as far as C.H. II would take the company. His tightfisted fiscal controls served the company well—until the mid-1980s.

Reinventing the Corporation

As a child, Chuck was enamored of tales of his great-grandfather and developed a sincere reverence for the family tradition. As a teenager, he worked in the warehouse and watched his father pore over corporate ledgers. In his mind, there was never a question that he would one day take the helm.

> *I knew that I would be a part of this business by the time I was seven.*

After earning his M.B.A. from the Wharton School—graduating in the top 10 percent of his class—he passed up $60,000-a-year offers from Chase Manhattan Bank and Citicorp to work in corporate finance. His compensation: $27,000 a year, plus incentives.

The puny salary didn't faze him. He had waited a lifetime to make his mark on the company. In fact, his two-year stint as a banking associate at Chicago's Continental Illinois National Bank and Trust Co. and his B-school credentials were all part of his plan. Besides, no one else from his generation was interested: His three sisters—Sheila, Stephanie, and Sarah—all sought to pursue other professions.

But, when he came back home in 1985, the market was spoiled.

The rise of supermarket chains, food cooperatives, and discount food warehouses in the early 1980s had put the squeeze on West Virginia's mom-and-pop grocery stores. Suppliers like C. H. James got caught in the pinch, forcing sales to slide to $2.6 million.

The son had seen the writing on the wall. He studied the dynamics of food distribution as part of his graduate school thesis. Now, as a corporate manager of the company, he wanted to put his theories into practice.

> *The strategy predicated on serving mom-and-pops was doomed, and basically that business on the wholesale side was tapering off quite a bit. Food distribution had gone the way of a lot of other industries. The big companies got bigger and the small companies went out of business. People in business find a formula that's successful, and it works for a period of time. When that period is over, they sometimes don't recognize it. If you don't know when to change your business formula, that is when you will be replaced by your competition. I didn't want [that to happen].*

So, the younger James quickly staked out new territory. Throughout its existence, out of pride and mere habit, C. H. James & Son had never engaged in competitive bidding for contracts or joined the 8(a) program, sponsored by the Small Business Administration (SBA), that set aside business for minority concerns. First, the new vice president gained certification as a government supplier. Then, he began networking with officials from minority supplier groups and talked with officials about the availability of contracts from such agencies as the Veterans Administration, the Department of Defense, and the like. C. H. James had a major advantage over other minority firms. Unlike in construction and janitorial services, there weren't many black-owned companies in food distribution—and none had a 100-year track record. All that was left for James to do was spend long hours completing inch-thick applications.

By 1987, he was named president, but his decisions still had to be green-lighted by his father. C.H. II wanted to stay the course. Chuck's new ideas would be implemented slowly—too slowly, he believed, for the company to survive.

Their business styles clashed. Chuck was a strategic consensus-builder not averse to taking risks. C.H. II was a steadfast numbers man with a conservative bent. Although his father's approach enabled the company to build substantial cash reserves to shelter it from stormy times, Chuck saw a tsunami coming that would wipe out his legacy.

He eventually had a candid conversation about the management structure.

"Daddy, did you run the business the way that your daddy did in the forties and fifties?" he asked.

"No," C.H. II replied.

"How do you expect me to run it today based on a formula that was successful more than 20 years ago?"

The elder James pondered the question.

Unfortunately, the answer came in the form of a life-threatening event. In 1988, C.H. II suffered a severe heart attack. After running the business for more than 25 years, he was compelled to step down. At 57, he decided to liquidate the company as a means of amassing enough funds for a comfortable retirement.

Of course, there was no doubt that Chuck would step up, deciding that he would be the only one to acquire his birthright. C.H. II was agreeable, but pointed in his intention to get all the cash he could. "You're welcome to make an offer," he told his son, "but I'm not giving any paper back."

The son engineered the sale through a leveraged buyout. He met with officials at Commerce Bank, the third largest bank in West Virginia, and arranged a $1 million 10-year senior note. James benefited from the fact that the bank had conducted business with his family for years and had already given C. H. James a $5 million line of credit. He paid his father in cash, and continued to use him as an adviser.

It was now Chuck's turn, at the tender age of 29, to be the head James in charge. He was nothing if not prepared.

> *My biggest challenge was establishing credibility. The employees remembered me as a kid running around the offices and, even though I purchased the company from my father, they knew I was there because I was his son. I had to make people take me seriously. I was just 29 years old and looked five years younger. I was making deals and people saw this kid whose skin still broke out. First of all, I had the business school credentials and I worked for another company. You should never go straight into a family business. Build your reputation at another company first. That way you are more likely to gain the respect of the employees that you inherit when you take over. But it took years of building their confidence with each success and each resolution of conflict. In The Prince, it says that a prince gains esteem through great deeds. Turning around the company would become my great deed.*

The Ivy League hotshot sought to establish a more professionally run environment—one with a mission statement, streamlined operations, training programs, and performance incentives. This would not be his father's C. H. James.

With the enormous competitive threat, he needed a strong, committed workforce. He had started the process of shifting the company out of its mature and declining market. Five out of nine of his major competitors had already bit the dust. C. H. James had to be nimble, an agile entity in a rapidly changing marketplace.

First, he carved out the 8(a) business (i.e., a program established by section 8(a) of the Small Business Act of 1953). By doing so, Chuck was making two bets: He was generating capital for the company outside of its base;

and he was giving C. H. James experience that it needed to tackle national and international accounts.

> *It didn't take long to see that mom-and-pop stores did not provide volume. I saw that 8(a) contracts were a quick way to get some. But I knew it was a time bomb because we saw so many businesses that became hooked on the program. Once their contract was over, they were done. It is a good revenue generator, but it certainly was not the long-term strategy for our business. On the other hand, I felt that we should take it while it was available to us. We could use it to build our capital base. We would continue to keep our eye out for an investment that would enable us to grow to the next level. I never viewed the company as a local business selling food in Charleston. I always saw it as a base from which to build an international food distribution business.*
>
> *The two people who helped me most during this period were Bill Williams, who inherited a printing business from his father, and Gaston Caperton, a successful businessman who eventually became the governor of West Virginia. With Bill, I discussed how to make the transition into the leadership role of my father's business. We shared the same issues of transition and building confidence in our customers and vendors and employees. The key was getting to know them and to make sure that you were consistent in performance and action. Bill told me that I quickly had to set the tone for my company. Gaston, on the other hand, told me to go to my industry's trade association and seek out the most successful member. He said that since I was a young upstart in the business and not viewed as a competitive threat, he would probably open up to me. He was right.*

C. H. James III referred to the 8(a) business as "gravy on the meal." It nourished the company with a $1 million contract to sell juices, pears, and pork and beans to the Department of Veterans Affairs; a $2 million deal to supply goods to the United States Department of Agriculture each year; and, by the early 1990s, a $9.6 million contract to furnish canned goods to the military during Operation Desert Storm.

The successful completion of government contracts also gave Chuck the confidence to bid successfully on such private sector accounts as Marriott hotels and Bennigan's restaurants. By 1990, 18 months after he bought the company from his father, he was able to pay off the Commerce Bank note.

James was moving with torpedo-like speed, finding that he was able to trade on the longevity of the company and the family name. Banking and supplier relationships had been established over three generations. And, he used these credentials to develop valuable statewide connections, such as a board seat at Commerce Bank and the position of treasurer of the West Virginia Economic Development Authority. It didn't hurt that he was on a first-name basis with the governor and C. H. James stocked the produce pantry in the executive mansion.

In 1990, the recession dried up sources of capital for small businesses. If James was going to pursue national accounts he needed to generate money for salespeople, warehouse space, and the like. Talking to his coterie of advisers, James discovered a novel low-risk means of financing future acquisitions: consolidate the company's West Virginia accounts, which grossed $3 million in revenues, and spin them off into a separate operating division. To make the strategy work, he approached John Wendling, a family friend and retired businessman who had sold his wholesale meat and cheese distribution business. Wendling, 52, still itched to get back into the game. A joint venture served both of their agendas. Wendling purchased a 49 percent stake in C. H. James's local distribution business, and then served as president of the newly formed subsidiary, Wendling James Food Service. The company operated as a subsidiary of C. H. James and developed a "reciprocal relationship" with Dixie Provisions, Inc., a concern owned by Wendling's son. To reduce overhead, the two companies shared warehouse space, increased their buying power by making

joint purchases, and expanded product offerings by buying goods from each other at cost. With schools and other
local institutions as new customers, sales grew to $1.5
million. The two parts became a dynamic whole.

For James, it proved an ingenious move. It enabled him
to produce additional revenues; maintain financial and
operational control of his traditional business base; and,
because Wendling was managing the operation, have time
to focus on high-margin national accounts. It worked well
until 1992, when new 8(a) regulations forced James to sell
his majority stake, since the federal government didn't allow partnerships in the same industry.

Doing Business with the Golden Arches

James could have stuck with 8(a) business, but it was
stopgap. Plus, graduation could come as early as 1995.
Besides, he wanted mass. He had envisioned himself as a
deal maker, a buyer and seller of companies. But when he
called on chains for business, he was often turned away,
informed that he had to deal with their main offices in
Chicago and New York. His West Virginia contacts held no
weight in such situations. Yes, he joined organizations
like the National Minority Supplier Development Council,
a promoter of corporate purchasing programs, but he
needed to link with a chain with deep pockets and clout.
By late 1990, James sat down with his management team
to devise an 18-month timetable for further expansion
through an acquisition or a strategic alliance.

In the summer of 1991, serendipity took hold: His
client-to-be found him through the June issue of *Black
Enterprise* magazine. They reviewed the list of the top 100
industrial/service firms to identify a company in food distribution and processing, and C. H. James fit the bill. The
company turned out to be McDonald's, the largest fast-
food operation in the world.

> *What I had to grapple with was whether I was going to
> be like Gary Cooper in* High Noon *and go it alone or find
> partners. Partners work well if they give you access to*

capital and key decision makers. Ironically, just as some of our 8(a) contracts were winding down, our opportunity with McDonald's came along. Jeff Bailey, a purchasing manager, told me that the company was trying to diversify its supplier base and he wanted to know if we were interested in being a wholesale food distributor for the company. The next week, I met them in Chicago. What they were actually trying to do was build up a talent pool of companies that had capital, that McDonald's could be comfortable with, and [that] could handle new business. Bailey told me at that meeting, "We got you in the pool. Just hold on. We know that there are some opportunities that will be coming up."

Over the course of the next year, James examined other prospective deals while McDonald's conducted its extensive background search, examining his relationships with creditors and clients. In 1992, McDonald's was ready to bring C. H. James into the fold.

McDonald's has a unique relationship with its suppliers: Historically, the company has only dealt with vendors on a handshake basis and, in turn, has helped many grow by giving them access to financing and an increased flow of business. In the early 1990s, the fast-food giant sought the formation of a minority-owned business that would exclusively supply them with precut produce products. When its first candidate bowed out, James got the call.

He met with Bailey in a conference room at the Oak Brook, Illinois, headquarters of McDonald's.

Bailey asked James, "What do you think about supplying produce for McDonald's?"

Confidently, James replied, "I don't think that is much of a stretch for us. We can do it."

"Well, we don't want you just to supply it. We want you to process it and send it to our distribution centers. We want you to get together with a company in California. We believe that C. H. James is just the company that we have been looking for."

It turned out that McDonald's wanted James to acquire 51 percent of North American Produce (NAP), a $14 million division of $1.2 billion Golden State Foods (GSF), the closely held supplier of 15 percent of all of the lettuce and onions for McDonald's restaurants nationwide.

It was a heady move. The acquisition could easily require an investment of millions. Even for the risk-ready James, this would be a stretch. He wondered, *What would my great-grandfather do?*

James rustled through the family archives in West Virginia. He found a dog-eared copy of the January 1920 issue of a now-defunct publication, *The Competitor.* In an interview given by his great-grandfather, he found his answer: "Our competitors are kicking now because our business extends to the farthest reaches of the district and so long as we keep reaching out, they must necessarily do likewise."

James, like his great-grandfather, wanted to extend his reach. In fact, ultimately, he wanted to go global. North American Produce would provide both capabilities.

This company was set up to be an African American–owned company, but McDonald's and GSF had a falling out with their first partner. It's a good deal because they provide access to capital and the food processing expertise. You need that because it is much different supplying a large business than a small business. Larger companies want to know whether you have a microbiologist on staff, the type of lab testing that you conduct, or whether all your fixtures are stainless steel. You can't do this deal on a shoestring. The expectations of quality standards are extremely high. So, you need the capital and technical expertise. It is not the same as dealing with mom-and-pops. With the NAP deal, we acquired that infrastructure in one fell swoop. We were still doing some things in Charleston on a national basis through our 8(a) contracts. This deal, however, literally changed us into national players overnight because of the resources that were there.

With McDonald's serving as the middleman, James met with GSF's CEO James Williams to map out the deal. It would take a year to hammer out the details. James would own a 51 percent controlling interest of NAP and oversee the daily operations of the company as its president and CEO. GSF would retain 49 percent of the operation. The stake for McDonald's: NAP would serve as its sole vendor over the next three years. This portion of the agreement was completed on a handshake since McDonald's doesn't sign contracts with suppliers.

To facilitate the deal, the young strategist would have to take another leap: move C. H. James's corporate headquarters, which had been in West Virginia for 109 years, to California. At the same time, he capitalized NAP by forming a holding company.

If I personally took the money out of C. H. James to purchase NAP, I would have been taxed personally. If I declared a dividend to myself, I would have been taxed at both a personal and corporate level. We found that we could use a dividend exclusion if a corporation receives a dividend from another corporation. We set up a holding company to receive the dividend and then invested in the new company on a dollar-for-dollar basis.

James needed professional expertise to complete the NAP acquisition, unlike the smaller transactions in West Virginia. When he structured deals in the past, he'd work out the details and then bring in attorneys to draft the contracts. Mercer Cook, a longtime family friend and business adviser, and Kevin Westbrook, a Harvard-trained mergers and acquisitions (M&A) attorney, assisted him in negotiating the deal points. The agreement, for example, gave James the right of first refusal to purchase all of NAP as well as receive a seven-figure golden parachute if the partnership dissolved over that same period.

I found in a deal like this, flexibility is important. You can't focus on what you want. You have to focus on what will work for both parties. You look at the minor things that you can sacrifice so that it will enable you to obtain the whole. The guy that came before me came with some nonnegotiable points and they said, "We'll see you later." The lesson that I learned is that the first thing you do is get a mergers and acquisitions lawyer, someone who does this type of transaction all day, every day. Not your cousin or your brother-in-law who happen to have law degrees. The nuances involved are incredible. Unless you get someone who knows the business, you can get nailed fast. In every relationship there's going to be four stages—forming, norming, storming, and performing. When we reached the storming phase, our agreement was tight. There was a three-year deal to take complete control but I had irrevocable warrants to do that. GSF said that they wanted to have the right, if they didn't think we were working well together, to buy their interest back. I said, "That's fine, but it has to be for cause and narrowly defined." And, if we decide to part ways, the check was going to have to be a big one. Without my advisers, I wouldn't have developed a sound exit strategy. You never go into business without one. You should build your business and develop each transaction for the day that you will eventually get out of the business or sell it.

The deal was completed in January 1993. James had finally achieved mass. His operation delivered products to 2000 McDonald's restaurants west of the Rockies.

As the new head of NAP, James quickly made changes after spending hours in the plant, visiting growers, and reviewing the financials. Taking another chapter from *The Prince*, he fired some top managers and installed those who would be loyal to him. He spent roughly $1 million in the first 18 months by installing automated weighing and packaging equipment, which increased productivity by 40 percent by shredding and packing 30 million pounds of lettuce and onions per year. He brought in consultants to help employees develop time-saving production techniques, and established a leadership team, including the rank and file, to set goals and timetables.

To maintain a smooth relationship with GSF, he formed a seven-man board that included himself, three representatives, and three from GSF. James reaped several benefits from the partnership. In 1995, he teamed up with GSF to expand its international presence by acquiring 40 percent of GSF Australia, a Sydney, Australia–based offshore company that processes and distributes precut lettuce to McDonald's restaurants in New Zealand, Hong Kong, Singapore, and Indonesia. Soon, he picked up Wendy's International, Taco Bell, and Burger King as clients.

I had the opportunity to buy out GSF but because of the things that we are doing and trying to do, it would not make sense to dissolve the partnership. We had been able to gain access to capital because of our partners. When you look at all of the successful enterprises, they had to have some partners to grow or got capital from Wall Street. Growth can be very expensive.

As for the next generation, he will not force either of his preadolescent sons to join the family business. He hopes that they will decide to embrace tradition on their own. But, when it's time for them to make their decision, their father is certain that, as successful as it currently is, C. H. James will not resemble today's operation. It may have evolved into something else entirely.

In fact, James made a strategic divestiture of NAP, selling assets back to GSF and retaining the brand name and his new client base. The move secured his family's financial future and freed up capital to pursue other deals.

Every generation of the family business had to go about things in a different way because markets change and channels of distribution change. These days, I see myself as a buyer and seller of companies. I view that as the only way to grow. Right now, everything that I own is up for sale—if the price is right.

10

PERCY E. SUTTON: INNER CITY BROADCASTING CORPORATION

The Politician

PERCY E. SUTTON

Age: 77.

Birthplace: San Antonio, Texas.

Marital Status: Married 53 years to Leatrice Sutton.

Children: One son, Pierre, 51, and a daughter, Cheryl.

Education: Prairie View College, Hampton Institute, Tuskegee College, and Columbia and Brooklyn University Law School.

Entity: Inner City Broadcasting Corporation.

Established: 1971 in New York, New York.

Products: Radio broadcasting, cable TV, TV production, and satellite TV distribution.

Annual Sales: $51 million.

Number of Employees: 270.

First Job: Worked in various positions in family business.

First Business Venture: Stock investor.

Sutton's Basics: *To deal honestly at all times; give support to family and friends; give back to the community; show people respect; have patience; stay in the race.*

On Money: *I came to realize that white Americans accumulated wealth through investments in stocks and bonds, [so] I [put] every dollar I could find in stocks.*

On Aging: *Some friends of mine have gotten old because they do not try new things. I tried to be on the cutting edge of a variety of businesses and ventures, all at the same time. I continue to have my sense of adventure, my sense of being a daredevil.*

Regrets: None.

10

PERCY E. SUTTON: INNER CITY BROADCASTING CORPORATION

The Politician

I believe that you always have to stay in the race.

They call him The Chairman.

It is a term of endearment, honoring his many years of public service and his leadership of one of the nation's oldest, and most dynamic, black dynasties.

At 77, an age when most people have retired, Percy E. Sutton is still elegant in his bearing and going strong. Operating from his Harlem law office, his base for more than 45 years, he's been responsible for changing New York's political landscape and creating an institution in black business. It was Sutton who took a mom-and-pop radio station and spawned Inner City Broadcasting Corporation, the $51 million multimedia information, entertainment, and broadcasting conglomerate that it is today.

Even though he no longer presides over the company— chairman emeritus is his title today—the patriarch, whose tan bald pate is bordered by silver hair, continues to develop potentially lucrative ventures, from international communications companies to high-tech healthcare services. To make such strides, he continues to leverage his business acumen and his substantial political currency. Most of his activities lean toward uplifting African Americans in some fashion or include "his family"—longtime friends, siblings, and offspring. A staunch proponent of multigenerational wealth, Sutton has crafted a succession plan that offers an enlightening example for family-owned businesses.

Every inch the smooth, polished pol, Sutton speaks with a courtly, ministerial cadence. The tireless entrepreneur, who trained himself to subsist on only four hours of sleep, concedes that age and illness have slowed him. But age, he says, is also freeing. Having proven his resilience time and again, today Sutton embraces political bouts and business challenges without fear of risk or failure. He is also, happily, free of regret.

> *The thing that I like most about myself is that I can sit at a table and gamble with $500, win $10,000, get up, cash in my chips, and walk away. Even if I lose my original stake, there's never the thought of what might have been or what I might have done.*

From San Antonio to Harlem

The youngest of 15 children, he cultivated his business philosophy from the example of his forebears. His grandfather was a freed slave who made his fortune by building and selling shipping wheelbarrows. Though illiterate, he understood well the importance of business ownership, using his money to develop one of the first black-owned banks in Richmond, Virginia.

Sutton's father—whom he reverently describes as "a five-foot, four-inch man with jet black skin who walked as if he was ten feet tall"—carried on the business tradition. He seemingly did it all. He was principal of the town's black junior and senior high schools, a landlord, an investor, an entrepreneur, and an undertaker. He believed in vertical integration before it became a part of the business lexicon. In addition to handling burial services, he sold burial insurance, made caskets and garments for the deceased, and owned the vehicles that carried the bereaved to graveyards as well as a cemetery. He used his money to invest in real estate and construction, including land near the Alamo, which is now downtown San Antonio.

My father was involved in a variety of businesses and invested his money in others. Not all of his investments were successful. He used to say that he often got involved in enterprises in which he had the money and his partner had the experience and, by the time he left the venture, his partner would have the money and he would have the experience. But our family was never without money—even during the Depression when he had to sell some of his holdings. He made sure that his family would have access to opportunities even though we did not have social access in the segregated South. Another one of his practices was to give a portion of his money to black organizations that helped those he called "people with broken wings." He felt it was important to show all black people respect— regardless of their station in life. I remember walking behind my father as he went to collect rent money. I was always struck by the fact that he would address everyone by their surnames. Many of his principles— diversification, giving back to the community, showing employees and associates respect—I held on to in my personal, political, and business life.

Education was prized in the Sutton household. As a youngster, he was schooled by his family at home—and in the classroom. His mother, father, and six of his older siblings served as his grade school teachers. The lessons didn't stop there: The Sutton home was a frequent pit stop for traveling black intellectuals such as W.E.B. DuBois and George Washington Carver.

Despite all that learned inspiration, what excited young Percy most was the radio. He'd listen to radio programs for hours, learning about worlds yet to be conquered outside the Lone Star State. He'd walk around with a corncob pipe, pretending to be an announcer. The fact that there were no black radio announcers did not stop him nurturing a dream to become one.

In pursuit of new challenges, he ran away from home at the age of 12 and headed to New York City. Landing with family near Harlem, he found a job as a sweeper and dishwasher behind the Apollo Theatre. Although back home two days later, he became mesmerized by the energy and style of America's premier black community. Little did he know three decades later he would play a powerful role in shaping that community.

The Path to Politics

Sutton's adventurous spirit seemed to grow as he did. As a young adult, he parlayed an interest in flying crop dusters into an income as a stunt pilot.

> *My friend, Red Dawson, showed me how to fly an airplane and then got me involved in aerial stunts. He was one of those guys who could convince you to do just about everything. Skydiving taught me a great deal about taking risks and having faith. After you survive 700-foot jumps without knowing whether your parachute would open, you find that there is very little in life that makes you fearful.*

Sutton was disappointed when an illness grounded him, preventing him from flying with the famed Tuskegee Airmen during World War II. Instead, he served as a combat intelligence officer, a role he would repeat during the Korean War.

In 1945, Sutton would focus on building a career. Instead of becoming a teacher like most of his siblings, Sutton believed he could make a better living, and influence change, as a lawyer. Already married to Leatrice ("a beautiful girl who looks just like my mother"), he had a family to support. So, he toiled weeknights at the post office, worked for the subway system on the weekdays, and waited tables when he was not attending Columbia University Law School at night.

It was at about this time that Sutton realized that he wouldn't make his fortune through hard work and savings alone. Remembering his father's example, Sutton began investing in the stock market. Saving a few hundred dollars from his many jobs, he bought shares of such blue chips as General Electric, AT&T, and Coca-Cola.

> *I came to realize that the way that white Americans accumulated wealth was through investments in stocks and bonds. I never touched my savings for emergencies or my children's education. I used, however, every available dollar that I could find to put in stocks. I read the financial pages and books on the financial markets. I mostly chose those companies that I felt would stand the test of time. Many of them I held for as long as 50 years.*

In the 1950s, Sutton set up a law practice and recruited his brother, Oliver. Since he was a youngster, the Sutton family were on the front lines of the Civil Rights Movement. He continued the fight, organized freedom rides, protests, and boycotts, anything he felt advanced the cause of African Americans.

Through such activities, he began making a name for himself. At the time, Harlem's most prominent leaders were the charismatic Malcolm X and the outspoken congressman Adam Clayton Powell. But the young attorney gained some distinction as president of the New York NAACP, and through his association with the local Democratic club, whose emerging leaders included David Dinkins and Charles Rangel, New York's future mayor and congressman, respectively. They would become a tight-knit crew, linked together by comradeship, politics, and business.

> *We believed that blacks in New York would advance through the political process. [We] discovered that political power and economic power went hand in hand. These were the people who would play a role in running the city and the state. They used their clout to develop economic opportunities for blacks. Some of these enterprises would become the nation's leading black-owned businesses.*

But, in the beginning, Sutton couldn't get elected dog-catcher.

For 11 years, he would place his name on the ballot in the races for city council, state assembly, state senate. Each time, he was turned away at the polls. He was determined to keep running until he gained a seat, any seat. In 1964, at age 43, the Harlem attorney was elected to the New York Assembly.

In the end, two powerful forces worked in his favor. First and foremost, he was endorsed by a client, Malcolm X, who was by then one of the most influential men in Harlem. Second, he had effectively used another potent tool—the radio airwaves.

Sutton found his audience through WLIB-AM and WLIB-FM, a paired favorite of Harlem residents. During his campaign, he had become a frequent guest on the stations' talk shows, debating opponents and discussing such issues as employment, police brutality, and other pressing concerns. As he made numerous appearances, he began to wonder what it would be like not only to have access to the medium, but to *own* it.

Despite Sutton's involvement in politics and civil rights, the blood of an entrepreneur coursed through his veins. As far back as 1961, he registered more than 20 different businesses under the name of Inner City. In fact, he and his brother Oliver, who would later become a New York State Supreme Court justice, owned a chain of gas stations.

Not one to overlook an opportunity, Sutton made the most of his visits to the radio station. Periodically, he struck up conversations with station owner Harry Novick. As they chatted about a range of topics, Sutton would routinely steer the discussions to the mechanics of the running and programming of such an enterprise.

One day, Sutton told the radio magnate, "I always wanted to be a broadcaster. If you ever think of selling, I'd like an option to buy." Novick took note.

In the meantime, Sutton continued to use the radio as a bully pulpit. One of his more memorable performances came months before he won the election. A mindless act of police brutality triggered the devastating Harlem riots of 1964. As soon as bedlam struck, Sutton arranged airtime and became radio's calm voice of reason. He told listeners that he shared their frustrations but suggested, "We should talk about not burning things down." Harlem residents heeded his entreaties for civility. He had helped extinguish the flames.

Novick was impressed with Sutton's eloquence and effectiveness. A few days later, the businessman approached him and said, "Percy, you've got your option."

Sutton was beside himself. This was, after all, radio. In buying the stations, Sutton would fulfill a childhood dream and gain a measure of control in an industry that he believed held the ultimate power: the power of communication.

First, of course, he needed the money, and getting it would involve a Sutton campaign of another color. The price tag for the stations totaled $3 million: $1.9 million for the AM station and another $1.1 million for the FM station. It would take Sutton eight years to raise the capital. He did it utilizing his network of contacts, shrewd salesmanship, and access to newly installed programs designed to foster black capitalism.

At first, no bank would even consider giving him a loan for a radio station. So Sutton decided to campaign for dollars the way he went after votes. With his 24-year-old son, Pierre, then managing editor of the *New York Courier*, a black weekly, he enlisted more than 50 investors, including Jesse and Jackie Jackson, songstress Roberta Flack, jazz pianist Billy Taylor, Malcolm X's widow Betty Shabazz, and David Dinkins, a close friend who would later become the Big Apple's first black mayor. Some of the consortium believed in the concept so much that they put up their personal property as collateral. Simultaneously, Sutton successfully applied for funds from BanCap, a minority enterprise small business investment company (MESBIC) authorized by the Small Business Administration. After years of being rejected by area banks, he finally persuaded an official at Chemical Bank to loan the company the remainder. Having put up the majority of the funds, Sutton's family controlled more than 65 percent of the company's shares.

> *I was determined to buy the radio station. The black community needed one. I was able to convince a number of people that the radio station was important if black people wanted to have their voices heard. People made an investment not to make money on a station in Harlem, but they were interested in getting a piece of the media that had an impact on the community. It took a while but I had patience. I believe that you always have to stay in the race.*

A funny thing happened on the way to financing the station: Sutton became electable. In 1969, New York City voters made him Manhattan borough president, one of the most powerful positions in the city. It also gave him a seat on the Board of Estimate, which made decisions on the city's fiscal matters.

By 1972, the year Inner City Broadcasting Corporation was actually christened, Sutton was in no position to run it. So, his son, Pierre, stepped in as president, running the enterprise with counsel from his father.

Although most of Inner City's original 32 employees had to receive on-the-job training, Sutton successfully convinced Harold "Hal" Jackson, a former disc jockey who had hosted programs on three different stations in New York, to come aboard as an employee and a shareholder. Serving as the company's vice chairman, Jackson helped structure broadcast operations and educated employees—including the Suttons—about the radio business.

Next, the management team sought to create a formula that would distinguish it from the competition as well as boost ratings and, in turn, advertising revenues. In 1973, the Suttons changed their FM station's call letters from WLIB to WBLS and began the process of retooling its format. Popular New York disc jockey Frankie Crocker was hired as program director, and began to soft-sell products, play longer musical cuts, and adopt a more sophisticated on-air personality. The new WBLS, with its brand of hip, upscale music and black-oriented public affairs programming, originated the popular "urban contemporary" radio format. Broadcasters in cities across the nation took note of its striking success and began to imitate its innovative programming style.

WBLS became one of the leading radio stations in the country, and Inner City's cash cow. In its first five years, company sales shot up 465 percent, from $1.3 million in 1973 to $6 million in 1978. WLIB-AM, which maintained the same talk-show format that helped propel Sutton into political office, would stay in the red for a decade.

From Politics to Business

Through much of the 1970s, the elder Sutton was involved with Inner City on the sidelines. For instance, he grappled with such major municipal issues as the potential bankruptcy of New York City in 1975.

By 1977, he decided to run for the ultimate prize: the mayorship of the City of New York. He wanted to follow the example set by blacks in most of the nation's largest cities, including Atlanta, Detroit, Los Angeles, and nearby Newark. All had been triumphant in getting blacks elected to the top spot in city hall. Sutton, along with his Harlem power network, believed that lightning could strike in New York. But, even though they galvanized legions of minority voters, Sutton was unable to garner enough votes in the Democratic primary to stop then-Congressman Edward I. Koch. After conceding defeat, in 1978 Sutton was out of office for the first time in 13 years.

He returned to his Harlem law office, where he received a visit from his son, Pierre. The 30-year-old radio station president wanted the elder Sutton to take the helm of the company that he started.

"I could use some help," he said. "Most of the shareholders and board members are old enough to be my parents. There's just not a whole lot of faith in someone young enough to be your child."

Sutton agreed to step up as chairman and CEO. His newest campaign: to transform Inner City into a communications empire—one that would be around for generations to come.

Seeking New Frontiers

In the late 1970s and early 1980s, the financial strength of WBLS, which hovered at the top of the New York City ratings, allowed Sutton to gain access to bank financing to purchase five new radio stations. In a flurry of activity, he added to the company's holdings KBLX AM/FM in the San Francisco Bay Area, KLBS in Detroit, KUTE-FM and KGFJ-AM in Los Angeles, and KSJL-AM and KSAQ-FM in his hometown of San Antonio. Many of the stations were profitable from the start: KLBS in Detroit was No. 9 in its market; the Bay Area station was ranked No. 11; and in Los Angeles, the Inner City stations combined were No. 4 among 83 stations.

During this period, Inner City also purchased Amistad Electronics, a manufacturer of electronic circuit boards in Grand Prairie, Texas, and acquired 50 percent of Sheridan Broadcasting Network, the second largest black news network with 108 radio affiliates.

The acquisitions proved to be a boon for the decade-old company. In 1981, the Inner City group of radio stations were valued at $78 million and a number of majority-owned conglomerates made offers to buy its flagship station, WBLS, for as much as $15 million.

Sutton wouldn't sell.

As he expanded the company, he placed relatives, friends, and their children in key operating positions. He made no bones about making Inner City a private repository of opportunity for "his family."

Now the company was positioned for much bigger game. While serving his last term as borough president, Sutton had become well versed in the next communications frontier—cable television.

[As Manhattan borough president], I had oversight over the development of cable television. It presented

big opportunities for black entrepreneurs. Unfortu-
nately, there were a number of blacks in other cities
who allowed themselves to be used in what I call
"rent-a-citizen" schemes. Giant cable corporations
used black locals as partners and then, once the fran-
chises were in place, bought them out for relatively
small amounts of cash. I saw cable television as a
hungry tiger. There were plenty of areas where minori-
ties could involve themselves—advertising, marketing,
engineering, writing, producing, and, most impor-
tantly, ownership.

Sutton was determined that his company would own—
not rent—such a system. As early as 1981, he envisioned
cable providing such diverse services as centralized burglar
alarms, shop-at-home buying services, remote medical di-
agnoses, and college courses, as well as a smorgasbord of
televised entertainment offerings.

Inner City's pursuit of the lucrative cable franchise in
the New York borough of Queens pitted it against such giants as Westinghouse, Time Inc., and Warner Amex. But
winning the franchise in one of the more lucrative markets had as much to do with political talent as with his
ability to raise capital. Inner City, with its well-known and
well-spoken chairman, had an advantage over its faceless
corporate competitors.

In gaining the award of a third of the Queens franchise—which had the potential of reaching 220,000 mid-
dle-income families—the former Manhattan borough
president wooed members of a dozen community boards.
But after he won the franchise, charges were leveled
against Sutton that Inner City was selected as a result of
political cronyism. After all, the late Queens borough
president Donald Manes, one of the key people in grant-
ing the franchises, was a Democrat who served on the
Board of Estimate alongside Sutton. At the time, Manes
insisted that Sutton was granted the award because the
company was run by "bright individuals, very much involved in New York City, who have been very successful at
anything that they have touched."

Sutton himself asserted that the decision was made as

a way of not freezing out new players. Inner City represented, at the time, one of only 16 black-owned cable operators of the more than 4500 cable systems in the nation.

Besides, Inner City was primed to delve into the new medium. As the owner of seven radio stations, it had broadcasting expertise. The company's success—gross sales of $18.3 million in 1982—enabled Sutton to gain $300 million in commitments from area banks as part of its Queens bid.

By now, having dealt with everything from the city's fiscal crisis to bond issues on the Board of Estimate, Sutton knew the players on Wall Street well. Thus, Inner City's investment package was structured by L. F. Rothschild, Unterberg, Towbin, a leading investment banking firm. It was a complex deal that provided for coownership status between Inner City and National Black Network (NBN), the nation's largest black-owned and black-operated radio news network, as well as two majority investors that had a 15 percent share of the venture. The investment bank committed $300 million in 1981 when the Sutton group bid on the entire borough of Queens to wire some 700,000 homes. Months later, the consortium put up $120 million when it was awarded only a third of the franchise.

With southern Queens virtually nailed down, Inner City began looking at other markets with substantial minority populations that had yet to be wired. They included Cleveland, Chicago, Detroit, Philadelphia, Baltimore, and Washington, D.C.

Showtime at the Apollo

As the cable transaction played out, Sutton had a side deal taking shape that had less to do with new technologies than with old stomping grounds. In October 1979, the 69-year-old Apollo Theatre, the most famous entertainment house in black America, shut down because of neglect and dwindling box-office receipts. Sutton saw in the dilapidated theater not just a valuable city landmark, but an invaluable emotional landmark for black Americans and, indeed, for himself.

In 1981, he decided to rescue it; he and his brother, Oliver, bought the Apollo for $250,000. Obtaining the money to renovate the theater turned into another masterful campaign of political maneuvering and personal persuasion.

First, he met with bankers at Manufacturers Hanover Trust to put up 30 percent of the $9.5 million to rebuild the theater. Then the Sutton brothers tried to issue $5.4 million in bonds to convert it into a cable television and entertainment center. The project stalled, however, when the New York State Mortgage Agency failed to insure the debt. Undeterred, Sutton went to his political allies to receive government funding from other sources.

Black and Hispanic political leaders, backed by then-Governor Mario Cuomo, lobbied the New York State Urban Development Corporation to approve a $2.5 million loan. Sutton met with members of the Harlem Urban Development Corporation to get an additional $1 million loan. Another $1.5 million came from a federal Urban Development Action Grant administered by the city. To complete the financing, the two brothers personally invested another $2.4 million.

Like his other enterprises, Sutton's grand scheme for the Apollo called for the development of synergistic operations, one that would generate revenues from concerts and events, television syndication, and licensing. Today, its main by-product is a syndicated program, *It's Showtime at the Apollo*, which has reached 70 percent of American households for more than a decade.

Putting together the funds for a cable system and theater proved to be grueling, even for a man who can get by on just four hours of sleep each day. Sutton, however, put together these deals as he faced his greatest challenge: cancer.

In 1981, I discovered that I had bladder cancer. These were very difficult times as I tried to work on this major project while getting chemotherapy treat-

*ments. I kept my spirits up, but it was hard. I was
fortunate that it went into remission in 1983. Now,
I am dealing with cancer again. In 1997, I suffered
a heart attack. But I am not letting these ailments
keep me from developing new projects. As long as I
am still living, and my mind is agile, I continue to
press on.*

Dealing with the Challenges of the Future

As The Chairman confronted his life-threatening illness,
the need to prepare for future generations became quite
real.

Did Inner City have a clear transition of management?
What will happen to the family's assets? These were questions that plagued him as he underwent chemotherapy
treatment. He was, after all, responsible for the Sutton
clan, from New York to San Antonio.

In 1981, he met with his financial advisers to draft a
comprehensive succession plan. In the document, he
transferred control of the company to his son, Pierre, and
further stipulated that Inner City would provide significant management roles for his daughter, nephews, and
the offspring of his shareholders.

*I knew of the horror stories of the dissolution of family
businesses and the erosion of family wealth because
of poor succession and estate planning. I didn't want
that to happen to my family. I decided that I was going
to take a decade to train the next generation and pass
on my management philosophy. [During that time] I
gradually removed myself from the company. The succession process, however, was handled in two steps.
First, I handed over control of the company. Now, I am
in the process of handing over the management of the
Sutton family's investment portfolio, which includes
stocks and real estate valued at more than $50 mil-
lion. To protect these transactions from estate taxes, I
placed the family's assets in a living trust, which
holds title of the assets. Since I am the trustee, I retain*

complete control to buy, sell, transfer, or borrow against these assets. The trust document stipulates that my son will be the successor trustee.

Sutton officially passed the keys of the Inner City kingdom to his son in 1991. As the transition occurred, Inner City faced its greatest challenges. Today, a plethora of stations use the urban contemporary format and, moreover, majority stations have lured listeners away by hiring high-profile pop and hip-hop celebrities to serve as deejays.

During the late 1980s and 1990s, Inner City's New York stations—albeit profitable—lost younger listeners who tuned in to gangsta rap, with its violent and misogynist lyrics, on white-owned, black-oriented stations. Holding fast to its upscale programming, Inner City refused to air any music that it felt degraded African American listeners.

To further strengthen the company, Inner City sold stations in Detroit and Los Angeles for a total of $25.6 million. To boost revenues at other stations, Inner City made major format adjustments. For example, the San Antonio station run by Sutton's nephew, Charles Andrews, adopted a heavy-metal format for the city's grunge set. Failure to respond quickly to changes in the marketplace—especially in the New York area—has forced Inner City to play catch-up as other stations siphon its audience. Despite the competitive heat, the Suttons refuse to sell their two New York stations, now valued at $250 million.

The cable venture, despite its rocky start, has gone well. After being awarded the cable franchise in Queens, Sutton had to contend with eight years of lawsuits and broken agreements with bankers. In 1989, he finally restructured a joint venture with NBN Broadcasting to gain a 50 percent interest in Queens Inner Unity Cable Systems and control of the board. Sutton serves as chairman of the venture, with Inner City and NBN holding half of the board seats. He also realized the value of teaming with Warner Communications (a subsidiary of Time Warner, Inc.), which owns the other 50 percent of the system and holds the remaining board positions. The venture has become profitable for Inner City through monthly cable subscription fees and Pay-Per-View revenues.

Sutton's pride and joy—and thorn in his side—remains the Apollo Theatre.

In early 1998, Sutton became involved in an imbroglio over television rights. The Apollo Theatre Foundation, which controls the landmark, has an agreement with Inner City to receive 25 percent of the profits, or a minimum payment of $2.5 million over five years for the television program *It's Showtime at the Apollo*. Because Inner City owes the Foundation $4.4 million, it was at risk of losing the rights to the Apollo name. Also, New York's Republican state attorney general launched an investigation into alledged improprieties sparked by the fact that Charles Rangel, a senior Democratic congressman and longtime Sutton ally, serves as the Foundation's chair.

Tenacious and resilient as ever, Sutton fought back, holding a press conference to reveal the millions that his family poured into the renovation of the theater, which totaled $18 million over a decade. He cited how distribution fees eroded profits and asserted that the investigation was a way for Republicans to settle political scores with old-line Democrats. In August 1998, Sutton prevailed, winning the rights to the program for another five years.

Sutton's focus now is on international communications. He recently developed a new venture, African Continental Telecommunications Ltd. (ACTEL), which plans to lease a stationary satellite 23,500 miles above southern Africa. The satellite would permit mobile and fixed communications on 1667 channels in a region that encompasses Zimbabwe, Zambia, Mozambique, and Botswana. It would also enable the company to build a continent-wide wireless communications network.

To achieve this goal, Sutton will need to raise roughly $835 million through equity investors and the issuance of high-yield bonds. He seeks to raise additional funds through an initial public offering of its southern Africa subsidiary on the Johannesburg Stock Exchange.

How will Sutton mastermind his latest venture? Via the same formula that has made Inner City prosper: by tapping a national and international network of politicians and financiers, converting talented employees and managers into shareholders, and installing family members to oversee the details.

> *I have found that friends of mine have aged because they do not try new things. I continue to have my sense of adventure, my sense of being a daredevil. When I was younger, it was stunt flying and politics. Today, it is computer technology. I learned how to use my computer and I'm in the process of learning how to browse the Internet. I will continue to seek out new campaigns, along with the challenges and opportunities that they bring.*

DON H. BARDEN:
THE BARDEN COMPANIES

The Player

DON H. BARDEN

Age: 54.

Birthplace: Detroit, Michigan.

Marital Status: Married 11 years to second wife, Bella Marshall.

Children: One son, Keenan, 32, and a daughter, Alana, 7.

Education: Attended Central State University.

Entity: The Barden Companies, Inc.

Established: 1981.

Products: Casino gaming, interactive training, and real estate development; automotive light manufacturing in Africa.

Annual Sales: $140 million.

Number of Employees: 1600.

Mission: To develop a diversified portfolio of well-run, *highly* profitable companies.

First Job: Worked in mailroom at American Shipbuilding Co.

First Business Venture: Failed record shop.

Barden's Basics: *You must be able to supply customer demand, whether it's a service, a particular product, or meeting a price point.*

On Strategy: *Own businesses that don't require 100 percent of your attention and time so you're always available to spot and pursue your next opportunity.*

On Money: *I never knew how it would feel to have $100 million in cash. I must tell you that it felt better than sex.*

11

DON H. BARDEN:
THE BARDEN COMPANIES

The Player

I [always] look for businesses that make money while I sleep.

Don Barden uses whatever is at his disposal to get what he wants.

He is the kind of guy who makes his own opportunities. Sometimes, they come by way of strategy; at other times, by fate. Regardless of the timing, he plunges into a venture, milks it for all it is worth, and shows no sentiment about flipping it. Then, he's off to find the next venture—sort of like Indiana Jones in search of the next treasure.

By leveraging his experience, contacts, and money, he built more than a half dozen businesses from scratch. His savvy and tenacity took the Barden Companies, Inc. (BCI) from a $600,000 concern in 1981 to a $140 million powerhouse. For two decades, BCI has shed more skins than a snake: scoring big in real estate, then cable television, and, more recently, casino gaming, interactive training, and vehicle manufacturing. Roughly 85 percent of BCI's revenues, or $115 million, are generated from a riverboat casino in Gary, Indiana. The other 15 percent of the company's gross sales is derived from Barden International, a $13.1 million vehicle assembly operation in Namibia, Africa; NovaNET Learning, Inc., a $13 million instructional computer-assisted learning service; and a smattering of real estate and media holdings.

While building his personal fortune, Barden became a pioneer in areas where few African Americans ever got a chance to play, no less win. For example, he became the first black businessman to build a cable system for urban markets. More recently, his adventures in the gaming industry have made him the first black entrepreneur to own a casino corporation outright.

I have learned to look for businesses that make money while I sleep. I like to acquire any business that doesn't require an exorbitant amount of time and capital to turn it around. Yet, I want to be able to expand the core business. I have been able to do that with real estate, cable, and gaming. If you find viable businesses with solid management, you are not drained by the day-to-day operations. You can scope out other opportunities.

Dapper and trim at 54, Don H. Barden is an unflappable man who rarely raises his voice in public. But in the heat of battle, he's a cobra willing to strike out at anyone or anything to preserve one of his franchises. He operates from headquarters located on the 24th floor of the Renaissance Center, known to Detroit residents as the RenCen. His plush showroom-sized office comes complete with an expansive view of the city's riverfront. One wall is choked with photos of Barden with politicians and celebrities, wooden plaques, and awards of glistening crystal. An easel next to a circular conference table in the middle of the room displays a rendering of the Majestic Star Hotel and Casino, a recent conquest. In the far corner of the office, his desk and credenza are covered by neat, foot-high stacks of reports on past and present transactions.

He doesn't like to waste time. Just as in his long-ago lean days, lunch is likely to be a slice of pizza on the go. His front office door remains open as managers constantly file in and out with details on commercial real estate buys or updates on a possible casino acquisition. But, when necessary, he uses a second door next to his desk to make quick, discreet exits.

Lesson #1: Think on Your Feet

Perpetual motion is part of the Barden work ethic. It was drummed into him by his father, Milton. Growing up in the then-rural Detroit suburb of Inkster, Michigan, during the 1940s and 1950s, he remembers his father having to work several jobs to support his mother, Lenora, and 13 children. Young Don was the ninth child.

The household was a great environment to develop the entrepreneurial spirit. First and foremost, my father's example showed me that you must work hard if you wanted to get ahead. He worked full-time at the Chrysler plant. He also ran an auto repair shop, raised crops and farm animals, and built homes. He felt that you had to keep moving to find the next opportunity. Secondly, in a household of 15 people, you had to learn how to get resources—food, clothing, and the like. You had to learn how to fight and cajole and find a way to hold on to what was yours. At the same time, our home was supportive and nurturing.

Barden always looked for ways to stand out from the crowd. He wouldn't just want to settle for being the quarterback and captain of the football team; he had to excel at basketball as well. After graduating from high school in 1962, he attended Central State University, a predominantly black college in Wilberforce, Ohio, and earned money during his freshman year as a barber in the school's dormitories. Unfortunately, grooming his classmates did not provide enough cash to pay tuition for his sophomore year.

In 1963, he moved to Lorain to live with his brother. During his first two years there, Barden worked at every type of job imaginable: laborer for a plumbing and heating company, shipping clerk, and cafeteria manager.

While I was working all of those different jobs, I realized that money and power gave you respect in this society. If I was going to control my destiny, I was going to have to take some risks.

Don Herbert Barden was about to learn his hardest lesson.

In 1965, the 21-year-old saved $500 from his slew of odd jobs and launched his first business: a record shop. Noticing how teens grooved to the Motown sound and other popular music of the time, he figured it to be a sure bet. In the era of vinyl records, all Barden had to do to be successful was sell volumes of 45s. Or so he thought.

Over the next three years, his small storefront business didn't exactly boom, but he survived, hawking enough records to pay the rent while earning additional cash through concert promotion.

But, in 1968, his operation was flattened by a steamroller of a business called Kmart.

> *It was quite a struggle trying to keep the business going. When Kmart opened up a few blocks from the location, it killed our business and a number of mom-and-pop operations. They sold records at half-price. Their loss leader was my bread and butter. On top of that, they had aisles and aisles of other products. We just couldn't compete. I was forced to sell the business. From that experience I learned that you must be able to supply customer demand, whether it's a service, a particular product, or, in this case, meeting a price point. You have to know what the customer needs or wants [and] be able to make a quick adjustment.*

Bloodied but not defeated, Barden started a public relations firm, which led to what he still describes as "the toughest period of my life." Its meager earnings supported an existence that fell more into the "survival" than the "lifestyle" category. It became clear that if he didn't find a sizable client, his second entrepreneurial endeavor would go bust, too.

Barden got his big break on a routine walk to the post office. He noticed military recruiters preparing to move out of their leased space. When he asked why they were leaving, an officer explained that, with the escalation of the Vietnam War, the military was beefing up its push for volunteers. To achieve that end, the recruitment center needed to be in a high-traffic pedestrian area.

From that brief exchange, Barden found out that the U.S. General Service Administration was coordinating the search for new space. He phoned immediately.

"I hear that you are looking for a new recruitment center."

"Yes, we are," replied the GSA official. "Do you have a building?"

"No, but I can find one to accommodate you."

Barden scoured Lorain, looking for the right site. Within a week, he not only found a location, but placed options on several buildings. The GSA reviewed them, selecting one in the town's commercial hub. The deal was set. Now all he needed was the money to buy the building.

Armed with a proposal and pictures of his potential acquisition, Barden went to Lorain National Bank and introduced himself to Stanley Pijor, one of the loan officers.

"I need a loan for $30,000," said the anxious Barden, showing the banker his pictures. "I need $25,000 to buy the building and another $5000 for capital improvements."

Pijor asked the wannabe real estate mogul whether he had collateral. "No," Barden admitted. "But the federal government is my tenant."

After further discussion, Barden's confident powers of persuasion and the GSA's clearance enabled him to seal the deal. Two years later, Barden sold the building for $50,000.

> *It was a perfect example of the supply-and-demand process. I knew exactly what my customer—the military—wanted and I got it. I owned the building and received enough from the lease to make mortgage payments. I was able to rent additional space in the building so I was able to show a profit before I sold it.*

In addition to meeting his client's needs, Barden discovered a workable model for future deals: Identify valuable properties and flip them for a handsome profit. To gain access to prospective ventures and the necessary capital, the entrepreneur would forge strong relationships with powerful decision makers. For example, Pijor, who would eventually become Lorain National's CEO, furnished him with a number of real estate loans over the next 20 years.

Lesson #2: Never Blend into the Crowd

Barden learned a great deal about taking chances from his initial business ventures. During the early 1970s, he diversified into a variety of vehicles—as many as time and stamina would permit. For five years, he ran the *Lorain County Times*, his small weekly newspaper where he wrote the stories, sold ads, and made deliveries to subscribers. (He launched the publication by convincing an insurance executive and George Steinbrenner, the pugnacious future owner of the New York Yankees, to grant him a $10,000 loan.) He used that position to meet a number of the town's most prominent businesspeople and learn about their companies by picking their brains over lunch and poring over financial reports.

Barden started to obtain a measure of exposure in his own right. He was hired as an anchorman and talk show host for a local television station in Cleveland, Ohio, spending 11 years on the air. Shortly thereafter, he became the first African American to hold a post in local government when he was elected to city council in Lorain, Ohio. He further expanded his sphere of influence by finding time to be involved in such diverse outfits as the NAACP, the Fraternal Order of Police, and the local chamber of commerce. He even organized a voter registration drive for blacks in Lorain County.

And so it went. The activities raised his profile to the extent that he was made a member of the one of Lorain's exclusive country clubs, a setting where he schmoozed the power elite.

> *I always used every position as a springboard for the next. My political experience gave me an insider's view to how decisions were made within local govern-*

ment and the ability to deal with a bureaucracy. My involvement with the newspaper and television taught me how to effectively handle the media. Also, I gained access to people [from whom] I could learn about the dynamics of different businesses.

As Barden juggled his growing array of jobs, he kept his hand in real estate development. True to form, he bid on projects that had an anchor tenant, usually a government agency. He didn't want to get stuck with a useless property and few available tenants. Moreover, he competed only in Ohio and Michigan, markets where he had developed contacts and a solid reputation.

As his confidence grew, he started bidding on bigger and bigger projects. In 1976, he zeroed in on Inkster, his old stomping ground. No longer the rural town of his youth, the now sprawling city needed facilities to house its Department of Social Services. Barden bought land, then developed and negotiated leases for a 30,000-square-foot complex—his first $1 million real estate deal. Two years later, he owned, developed, and leased a 75,000-square-foot Veterans Administration facility in Canton, Ohio. Project cost: $3.2 million.

He would continue to purchase and lease buildings until he developed a portfolio worth roughly $6 million. In tandem, Barden expanded his sphere of influence, which came in handy when he set his sights on cable television.

Before MTV introduced music videos and CNN created the global village, cable was largely a suburban phenomenon. In the late 1970s, fledgling companies were looking for ways to pump out programming to middle-class Americans who migrated from the urban core to outlying communities of metropolitan areas. Most companies went after these "plums"—franchises outside major cities where income levels were relatively high and construction costs were low. Barden, however, believed that urban America offered more digestible fruit.

To harvest these communities, he needed to get his hands on the seeds. Barden, who lost his bid for a seat in the Ohio Senate, had maintained his local business and political contacts. By 1981, after two decades of building relationships and credibility, he was ready to use his power to ensure that African Americans gained an equity participation in cable franchises in Lorain and nearby Elyria. He negotiated for blacks to receive a 4 percent interest in both operations, becoming one of the chief beneficiaries. Using $4000 of his own money, he purchased a 2 percent stake in each of the franchises. Two years later, he sold his interest for $200,000, earning a staggering 5000 percent return on his investment. Those were the type of figures that excited him.

He had to get wired.

A lot of major companies were afraid to bid in black markets. They thought the tires would be cut in alleyways. They had a misperception of the market. They didn't do their homework. I started filing for rights to construct cable systems in as many African American communities as possible. Of course, I looked at Inkster and Detroit but I put in applications as far [away] as Seattle and Compton, California.

In 1981, Barden used his close community ties and impressive business track record to snare the Inkster franchise, wiring 10,000 homes in the city. A year later, he gained the rights to Michigan's Van Buren Township, and Romulus a year after that. Those franchises launched Barden Communications, Inc., which consisted of Barden Cablevision; a radio station in Coal City, Illinois; and Cable Cheque, Inc., a merchandising incentive program similar to Home Shopping network.

But what made Barden a major player in cable was his acquisition of the Detroit franchise. By 1982, Detroit had followed other major cities and started its cable system award process. Barden saw it as his big chance. He spent $500,000 in personal funds and credit lines to pay for the eight-volume cable system proposal. In 1983, Detroit's cable commission gave Barden's proposal and two others to an outside consultant. After evaluating them on a point system, the consultant selected Barden. Once he got the nod from Mayor Coleman Young and the Detroit city council, Barden won the rights to the cable franchise, a 15-year contract to construct and operate the system.

But Barden had to fight to keep the contract. The two firms that bid against him filed lawsuits claiming that BCI had received preferential treatment because it was the only minority bidder. A federal judge ruled that there was no indication of favoritism in the case. What worked to Barden's advantage was that he had the only Michigan cable television company that controlled an existing franchise. Moreover, as a Detroit-based company, five percent of the company's revenues would go to the city.

But he wouldn't escape further controversy. Local columnists criticized him for being "better connected" than the other bidders, alleging that his campaign contributions to Mayor Young's reelection campaigns gave him the edge. Others questioned the propriety of his personal relationship with Bella Marshall, who served as finance director in the Young administration. (Barden and Marshall were later married.) "I take firm exception to people implying that I got the franchise because I was the friend of the mayor," Barden said at the time. "I didn't know the mayor. I began dating my wife after the award as well."

A tougher—and more significant—challenge was raising $100 million to make 375,000 households cable-ready. After moving his corporate headquarters from Lorain to Detroit in 1984, Barden developed a short list of cable heavyweights as potential partners. He narrowed it down to Tele-Media, an outfit that had 530,000 subscribers at the time; Maclean Hunter (MH), a Toronto, Canada–based communications conglomerate that owns newspapers, cable television operations, and commercial printing; and Tele-Communications, Inc., the nation's largest cable operator, whose chairman, John Malone, is considered the most powerful man in cable (Malone is also a partner of Robert Johnson, CEO of BET Holdings, another B.E. 100s company. See Chapter 2).

I wanted to go with the company that gave the least amount of headaches but would provide capital and expertise. Those three factors always dictate whether I will enter a partnership. My partnerships have to be advantageous, required, and desirable. In most cases, I look for such arrangements where I have a controlling interest or at least an equal stake. We went with Maclean Hunter because they would give us the greatest strategic advantage.

Barden also wanted control, something that Malone, aka "The Cable King," wasn't about to give him. Sitting across the table from MH CEO J. Barry Gage, he spent hours hammering out the deal. It worked like this: Barden would sell 49 percent of the franchise, which was valued at roughly $25 million at the time, and retain a 51 percent controlling interest. To make the operation work, MH loaned Barden another $15 million, and introduced him to its bankers at Toronto Dominion Bank, which would arrange another $85 million line of credit.

The deal was classic Barden. He controlled the cable system, while MH arranged 100 percent of the financing and guaranteed a significant piece of it.

It took five years, from 1986 to 1991, and $120 million to lay 2100 miles of cable beneath downtown Detroit while stretching the remainder across utility poles within the metropolitan area. Additional funds were spent on buildings, personnel, and purchasing equipment needed to gather 78 channels. The additional $25 million cost—beyond the financing from the bank and MH—came from BCI's cash flow.

By the time the system was fully operational, the cable system was worth close to $300 million, and employed 322 people. As of 1992, BCI was tuned into 120,000 households, or 35 percent of all of the homes in Detroit.

It was a new environment for Barden. For years, he had run one-man shops or small enterprises. He adopted a decentralized management style, finding the best people for the job and letting them run with the ball. He would hold them accountable if they fumbled an assignment, but provided ample rewards when they scored.

Although the cable operations were successful, not all

of his ventures would be. In the late 1980s, he purchased the vacant Northland Inn Hotel in Southfield, Michigan, for $1.5 million. For more than four years, the hotel, which was to be converted into a senior citizens complex and retirement home, stayed vacant. Ultimately, he scrapped the project and sold the property at a loss.

In September 1987, he made another heavy investment, this time in First Federal Bancorp (FFB) in Pontiac, Michigan. According to Barden, the federal government made FFB invest $15 million in a failing Florida bank, which depleted the Michigan concern's reserves. FFB lost another $6.5 million in an alleged mortgage scam in 1989. By late 1991, the bank was placed under conservatorship by the Resolution Trust Corporation, the agency mandated to liquidate the assets of failed thrifts. Blaming the federal government for putting the thrift out of business, Barden lost about $1 million over a three-year period.

Although still preoccupied with the cable television business, he found time to develop his real estate interests. In 1988, Barden founded Waycor Development, Inc., a real estate development firm. Waycor's projects included the construction of a $10 million, 144-unit apartment complex in Detroit and the $64.5 million Wayne County Detention Center.

Lesson #3: Never Make the Same Mistake Twice

In 1994, Barden became restless again. He realized that cable had dramatically changed. Now, big players like Time Warner, TCI, and Bell Atlantic wanted to zoom onto the information superhighway and sought lanes to 500-channel outlets and converging technologies. He sold Barden Cablevision to the Comcast Group of Philadelphia after realizing that telephone companies and media monoliths would squeeze smaller operators, like him, out of the industry. Having learned from his first business mistake, Barden was not about to have his cable operation crushed in the same manner that Kmart put his record shop out of business. Barden's take this time: $115 million.

*I always wanted know how it would feel to have $100
million in cash. I must tell you that it felt better than sex.*

His next big venture was eight years in the making.
Back in 1986, Barden sat down to lunch with Mayor
Thomas Barnes of Gary, Indiana, and members of his
staff. Still reeling from the 1981–1982 recession, the city
fathers had spent the past few years trying to find viable,
new industries to replace the city's dependence on steel
mills.

Barnes had been impressed by Barden's success in real
estate and cable ventures and the economic boost they
gave to cities in Ohio and Michigan. The mayor asked Barden for suggestions on reviving Gary's ailing economy.

Barden quickly pointed to the city's undeveloped water-
front and, over the next several years, provided them with
free consultation on the matter.

In 1993, city hall officials concluded that the best way to
boost municipal coffers was with the roll of a dice. Taking
its cue from Atlantic City, Gary would offer casino gambling. Barden saw their plans as an opportunity to further
diversify his corporate portfolio. Casino gaming fit snugly
into his criteria. It was a potentially big moneymaker that
wouldn't require his constant oversight. But the scale of
such a project, like his cable operation, would require a
partner with deep pockets and casino business expertise.

*In 1993, I sought out President Riverboat Casinos of
St. Louis, which is the largest riverboat gaming company in the nation. We agreed to be equal partners
and split all costs associated with the venture. They
brought the expertise and a portion of the money,
while I had the relationship with the city. But this
business relationship did not go as well as the one
with Maclean Hunter. President Riverboat Casino ran
into serious financial trouble and was unable to come
up with half of the $30 million that was needed to de-
velop the casino and pay for slot machines and tables.
But I was fortunate. Just as they were about to bail
out of the deal, I completed the sale of my cable sys-*

tem. I was able to buy out their share and proceed with the venture. By December 1994, we were awarded a certificate of suitability for a license to own and operate a riverboat casino.

It took Barden three months to refurbish his leased riverboat. In June 1996, he finally opened the *Majestic Star*, which featured 932 slot machines and 50 table games. In its first five months of operation, the casino grossed $53 million.

Not surprisingly, Barden's success bred competition. Gaming impresario Donald Trump decided to develop a riverboat casino in the former rust belt city. The newly inducted riverboat gambler felt that he could increase revenues and "trump" the competition with a larger, state-of-the-art vessel. He sought to raise $105 million to build a 43,000-square-foot boat with gaming on three decks. The price tag? Roughly $50 million. The remaining funds would finance operations.

We went to the investment bank, Wasserstein Perella, to raise the money through high-yield bonds. I was scheduled to go on a road show to pitch the bonds in 20 cities over 11 days, which was an exhausting schedule. Within seven days, investors were so excited about the potential returns, we were $400 million oversubscribed. Lady Luck smiled on me. By October 1997, we water-launched the Majestic Star, *which is currently one of the five largest gaming vessels on U.S. waters.*

Lady Luck was not as kind when Barden tried to break into casino gambling in Detroit. In April 1998, he was embroiled in a bitter dispute with Detroit's mayor, Dennis Archer, to gain entry into the $2 billion casino business that promised to remake Detroit in the next millennium. He had officially lost his bid when the mayor granted three licenses to MGM Grand Detroit, controlled by gaming mogul Kirk Kerkorian; Detroit Entertainment, partly owned by Circus Circus; and Greektown Casino, whose shareholders include the Chippewa Indians.

But Barden refused to fold. The mayor's decision sparked a heated debate among some Detroiters who maintained that one of the licenses should go to a corporation with majority black ownership in a city where about 80 percent of the residents are African American. The natural choice, many of the protesters argued, was Barden since he was a local businessman. Some newspaper pundits maintain that he secretly initiated the public furor.

During much of the winter, Detroit's city council held special sessions to decide whether it should back the mayor. As usual, Barden was plugged in, receiving calls from his government sources and supporters. It was important for him to protect his franchise and expand his gaming operations, which currently generated about $2 million a week, on his home turf. In fact, he pledged to place a portion of casino revenues in trust, with the city as his beneficiary.

In a vintage political maneuver, he vowed before television cameras that he would "use all the resources available to me . . . [to] fight punch-for-punch, blow-for-blow." He subsequently received an offer to be a minority partner in one of the casino groups, but Barden refused to be a backseat player. Despite his efforts, the city council voted with the mayor.

Barden was down, but those who bet against him would live to regret it. In August 1998, large numbers of Barden supporters initiated a ballot question, but the mayor's decision was confirmed by voters on a narrow margin. The entrepreneur then teamed up with megastar entertainer Michael Jackson to announce their plans for Majestic Kingdom, a $1 billion casino, hotel, theme park, and resort on Detroit's waterfront. With Michael Jackson at his side, Barden's local victory became national news.

Lesson #4: Set Your Terms, and Stick to Them

Although he has been based in the Motor City for 14 years, Barden was never attracted to the automotive business. The industry, with its dependence on fashion trends and the economy, simply did not fit his criteria.

Ironically, he got into the auto business by way of Namibia. In 1995, Barden served as host to Sam Nujoma, the president of the southwestern African country, who was on an official visit to Detroit. Among the dignitary's many stops was a visit to General Motors.

When a GM official pressed Nujoma about business opportunities for GM in his country, the dignitary began to list his prerequisites. First and foremost, he demanded jobs for his countrymen. Then, he looked the official square in the face and said: "We'll only do business with General Motors if Don Barden is involved."

Barden was taken completely by surprise. He became intrigued by the prospect but remained wary of the automotive business; he didn't want to fall prey to the fickleness of consumers or a recession. He agreed to build a facility only if he got a commitment from the Namibian government that they would buy cars from him. He then struck a deal with GM to have his new company, Barden International, as an authorized dealer and distributor to sell North American–made trucks and cars in Africa. The total value of the deal: $150 million over five years.

With a locked-in agreement, Barden committed to construct a $13 million plant that would handle the retrofitting and distribution of vehicles. Future plans include exporting vehicles to other countries in southern Africa.

Lately, Barden seems driven to leave a larger imprint on society. After his brother, Bernie, a manager at a Ford factory, was fatally stabbed in 1991, Barden was inspired to develop "economic peace summits" to get Detroit's private sector more involved in reducing the city's crime rate, improving its image, and fostering economic development. He was so engaged that many viewed him as one of the front-runners for mayor of the Motor City. He scoffs at the notion: "I'm a businessman."

His investment in NovaNET grew out his interest in education. He was intrigued when the company founders told him about the potential of computer learning systems and software services for the educational market. In

1995, he purchased a 52 percent stake in the Tucson, Arizona–based company for $1.5 million. Over the past few years, more than 100,000 students have received 2 million hours of instruction.

While that statistic makes for great public relations, Barden is the first to admit that his investment was not based on corporate altruism. The company has been growing at a clip of 30 percent a year.

"This is something for the future," says Barden the politician, playing, as always, to his public.

"Then again, it's not a bad business." That's Barden the entrepreneur talking. Loud and clear.

Acknowledgments

I am indebted to a number of people who made major contributions to the development and completion of this book. I am especially grateful to the following:

The Titans of the B.E. 100s, many of whom let me spend hours and days with them. They told their stories in their own words and gave me the chance to watch them conduct business. The experience was educational, exciting, and inspirational. My heartfelt thanks and admiration to John H. Johnson, Robert L. Johnson, Clarence O. Smith, Russell Simmons, Byron E. Lewis, Mel Farr, Sr., Emma C. Chappell, Herman J. Russell, Charles H. James III, Percy E. Sutton, and Don H. Barden.

The staff of the Titans, who spent hours and days coordinating schedules and phone calls so that I could gain insight from these dynamic entrepreneurs. They are Lydia Davis Eady of Johnson Publishing Company, Inc.; Michele Moore of BET Holdings, Inc.; Annetta McKenzie of Essence Communications, Inc.; Simone Reyes of Rush Communications and Affiliated Companies; Lynn Wilson of Uni-World Group, Inc.; Charlene Mitchell and Kim Crawford of Mel Farr Automotive Group, Inc.; Mary Anne Bartley and Claudia Averette of United Bank of Philadelphia; Iris W. Register of H. J. Russell & Company; Kimberly Shew of C. H. James & Son Holding Company, Inc.; Sylvia Schoultz, assistant to Percy E. Sutton; and Angela Bell of The Barden Companies, Inc.

Ruth Mills, my editor at John Wiley & Sons, who appreciated the book idea and spent many hours shaping this tome into one that would be both instructive and compelling. Her assistant, Kirsten Miller, ensured that the process kept flowing. I thank you both.

Missy Garnett and the crew at Cape Cod Compositors, who spent weeks copyediting and typesetting this manuscript, under the direction of Sasha Kintzler at John Wiley & Sons.

Friends and family members, who were there during some rough spots. Thanks to James Hughes, Dwayne McDuffie, Robin McCallum, Roger Tucker, Sheryl Hilliard, Joanne Barham, and my brother and sister, Butch and Velda. A special debt of gratitude is owed to my grandmother, Blanche Spruill; my younger brother, Kevin; and, of course, my mother, Mattie—without their contributions this book would not have been completed.

The *Black Enterprise* family, who have always provided encouragement, guidance, and support. My personal gratitude to my role model and mentor, Earl G. Graves, Sr., a man whose vision and energy were responsible for the development of the B.E. 100s and cultivating a generation of entrepreneurs and professionals—including myself. Special thanks to Earl "Butch" Graves, Jr., John C. Graves, and my brother Alfred Edmond, Jr., who allowed me to pursue this once-in-a-lifetime project. I would also like to thank Tanisha Sykes, who handled the awesome task of fact-checking this book with speed, enthusiasm, and grace, as well as the rest of the *Black Enterprise* staff.

Caroline Clarke, editor of B.E. Books, who selected me for this project. She provided me with encouragement and much-needed prodding, and applied her considerable editorial skill to make this book much better than I could have ever imagined. Most important, she continued to believe at a time when many would have thrown in the towel. You have my unyielding gratefulness.

Lastly, the B.E. 100s, past and present. Your stories continue to inspire today's black entrepreneurs and generations to come. I was honored to play a role in chronicling your adventures and achievements.

INDEX